Mongolia or Bust

A round-the-world motorcycle misadventure

David Newman

Copyright © 2015 David Newman

All rights reserved.

ISBN: 1517186722
ISBN-13: 978-1517186722

To my wife Helen, who always believed.

Contents

Why Go 11

The Route 13

The Bike 15

Paperwork 22

Preparation 24

UK 36

France 38

Italy 48

Slovenia 54

Croatia/Bosnia 56

Montenegro/Albania 59

Greece 62

Turkey 65

Georgia 77

Azerbaijan 79

The Caspian Sea 84

Turkmenistan 90

Uzbekistan 99

Tajikistan 105

Kyrgyzstan	115
Kazakhstan	122
Russia	132
Mongolia	136
Ulaanbaatar	149
China	157
USA	166
California	174
National Parks	177
Presidents	186
Pilgrimage	191
Reflections	215
Does it change your life?	219
References	220

Preface

I wrote off my first motorcycle in an unfortunate incident with a rabbit before I had even finished making the loan repayments. One early morning, full of excitement, I was riding from my home near Newcastle towards Liverpool to catch a ferry to the Isle of Man. It wasn't Tourist Trophy (TT) week but the lure of the unrestricted mountain road had tempted us to go for the weekend. On the way up the infamous Hartside pass near Alston in Cumbria, the air was still cold but it was bright and sunny. I saw the rabbit run out in front of the bike I was following. It narrowly missed going under the wheels of the lead bike, but instead of carrying on to safety on the far side of the road as I expected, the bunny gracefully arched its run back towards my side of the road. The delay in me hitting the brakes proved fatal, as just at the point where I wanted to turn into the next right hand bend, unlucky bunny went right under my front wheel causing a wobble and making me stand the bike up. I probably had time to turn in again, but inexperience and thoughts of the side of my tyre being covered in rabbit guts meant I ran wide onto the grass verge. Unfortunately the verge was soft and the front wheel dug in, tipping the bike over and me off. I rolled off unhurt, but the bike was not so lucky. The front fairing was broken and the radiator twisted. Having picked it up, I ascertained that the bike still ran. Having taped up the damage I carried on for the weekend on the island. This included several high speed runs over the famous mountain road, hitting speeds of 120mph plus. It wasn't until I returned home that I rang the insurance company, and subsequently found out that the bike was beyond economical repair.

In 2007 I had the idea to go on a biking holiday. I recruited Al, whom I knew from my job and we flew to Portugal where I'd arranged for a local bike hire company to meet us at Faro airport. We rented two little

Yamaha DT125 dirt bikes, one black and one blue. We'd booked the first few nights in a hotel in Quarteria with the idea that we might travel a bit, so leaving the remaining nights open. In the end we realised that the bikes were so underpowered that travelling any great distance on main roads would be a boring and painful experience. Instead we booked the remaining nights at nearby Villamoura where the night life and surroundings were a lot nicer. The harbour area was full of pleasure yachts and lined with bars and restaurants. Instead of travelling far we concentrated on finding and exploring dirt tracks through the hills of the Algarve. Despite, or perhaps because of, their lack of power, the bikes were perfect for us off road novices. Their light weight was confidence inspiring and we spent time practising our riding around an old quarry we found. The weather was variable but we had a great time, even though the two stroke bikes proved less than totally reliable and having to call on the hire company to come and replace an oiled up spark plug. The bikes were kick start only and could take a bit of getting going. We found cafés to buy lunch away from the developed coastal strip where nobody spoke English. Very limited Portuguese meant successful ordering amounted to ham and cheese sandwiches! We spent the evenings exchanging stories of near crashes, pot-bellied pigs and rabid dogs, all over ice cold lagers. We overcame incidents like the bike chain coming off the rear sprocket and a bout of overconfident riding from me, resulting in pitching the little bike into a ditch at the side of the road. Thankfully there was no damage other than adding a few scratches to the already tired looking bike. I road on sand for the first time on the beach and put into practice the techniques I'd read about. This holiday really set the seed in our minds of how good it would be to ride and travel every day for months at a time. Each day seemed exciting, dramatic and new.

I have read a few motorcycle travel books where the trip in question was just a couple of weeks holiday or I thought the author really didn't do a very good job. Having written a book of my own I realise it isn't as easy as some people make it seem. I hope you enjoy my efforts. It took me over four years since the end of my journey to make a start on writing. I'd never intended to write a book and I have a lot of mixed feelings about the journey itself. I don't often talk about it, and have never really spent any time looking through photographs or mementos. In that context, writing a whole book seems to me a bit odd.

Why Go

I'd always liked travel and the excitement of heading off to unknown places. However, I'd not had a gap year from university and gone backpacking as many people do. I'd felt on some level that if I had a gap during my education I'd never be able to come back and return to studying. I was also very keen to get into a good job. I wanted independence in the form of buying my own house, and of course being into cars and motorbikes, you need money to feed the habit. So I did just that. By the time I'd finished my masters I had a place on a graduate scheme secured. Over the coming years I bought the house and the sports car and the shiny road bike. I enjoyed them, but the work gradually wore me down with a mixture of boredom and an irrational fear that someone would eventually rumble that I was faking, that I wasn't really worth the money or good at my job. I say irrational now, because there was never any indication that there was anything wrong with what I was doing. Being bored led me to the internet, and eventually reading about the adventures other people were having all over the world made me constantly consider if I was wasting my life, my one opportunity, staring at a computer screen. Being a motorbike fan, the overland trips captured my imagination. The combination of travel and spending each day riding sounded fantastic, and the idea of taking off and leaving it all behind just wouldn't go away.

An early mid-life crisis is how I often think of it. One crisis point in a sea of feeling that one should be doing more. It is the destiny of the atheist, I believe, to worry on some level about whether or not they're making the most of their time. That's the trouble with not having a heaven, an afterlife or a reincarnation to fall back on. One of my favourite phrases is 'if not now, then when'. Let me explain. It's a motivator; for everything I want to do or achieve I try and remember to do this test. I think about whether there is a legitimate reason why there will be a better time in the future to do this activity or achieve this goal. There rarely is. In this case I was still unmarried and had no children. I was also in a career which was making me stressed. Now pushing thirty it seemed unlikely that life would get any less complicated in the future and so the answer was clear. Now is the time. Not only that but every article you read or news item you see describes how some environment is being destroyed or culture disappearing. It seems as though most places you would go and see on a world tour are as good as they're going to get. You've probably missed the golden age of most things, so best get out there now before the rest follow suit! There lies the sense of urgency required to overcome the status quo, the inertia of friends, and family and jobs and houses and normality. The opportunity was there also, someone else wanted to go. People you know who want to disappear off around the world on a motorbike are pretty thin on the ground. And when ideas are discussed, not just festering in the mind of one person, they gather a kind of momentum that is fuelled by bravado and collective madness. So that was it, Al and I were going to set off on the trip of a lifetime.

The Route

Deciding on the route is probably the most fun part of planning any road trip. We could have gone anywhere, but decided fairly early on to set off from home. This sounds obvious, but one idea was to fly to another continent, buy motorcycles once there and set off. This idea was shelved in favour of being able to buy and prepare the bikes in familiar surroundings. Leaving from home on our main chosen mode of overland transport also felt right, and opened the possibility of one day arriving back home on the same machine. A short hop on a ferry or through the Eurotunnel would land us in Europe which would be a gentle introduction to foreign lands, but then where? Africa seemed war torn and problematic, with many reports that different routes were impossible due to various ongoing diplomatic disputes resulting in closed borders and no-go areas. So going south was out, leaving us with various Easterly routes to choose from.

I wanted to go to lots of countries with different cultures; especially ones where people from the UK don't often go. It is possible to get from the UK almost to the other side of the world in far east Russia using just European Union countries and Russia itself, but where's the fun it that! Iran seemed like the gateway to the east but unlike other countries would require us to buy an expensive carnet, so it was eventually ruled out. In any case further border problems lay ahead in going further south through Pakistan and on towards China. Mongolia emerged as a must have on the route as I read of its reputation for wild open spaces, and a total lack of road network. Our route through Europe, the Balkans, the "Stans" and Russia towards Mongolia took shape as the collective knowledge of those who had gone before was gleaned from the World Wide Web.

Far from confident of a full circumnavigation, tentative plans were put in place to ship the bikes from eastern Russia to the USA via Korea, but no cash was committed or bookings made. I genuinely felt that the likelihood of getting that far was no better than 50/50. I almost expected that a trip ending accident or robbery was bound to occur. Nevertheless it felt important to me just to try, to go anyway, to take a risk. If you're in the planning stages, the good news is that in fact the vast majority of places feel much safer once you are there than when it is just an unpronounceable name on a map. Ride carefully and there is no reason there will be any problem. That's not to say there won't be challenges and memorable moments! I believe traffic is the most likely cause of an accident largely outside of your control on a trip like this. In that regard the most worrying moments were had filtering along the M25 motorway around London, still in England, on the very first day.

The Bike

Probably the most popular board on any motorcycle travel forum is which bike to take. Arguments rage, from brand loyalties and engine layout, to the never ending bike size debate. Then there is always someone who comes along and argues that it doesn't matter and you should just set off yesterday on whatever is already in your garage. For what it's worth here's the way it panned out for us. A common theme in the online discussions is that the in vogue bikes, the BMW GS1100 & 1200's, made famous and popular by the Long Way Round, with Ewan McGregor & Charley Boorman, were too big and heavy. I happen to agree with this because at 5'9 and about 145lbs I very much doubted that I'd be able to pick one up after I'd crashed it! This wasn't the main reason I didn't want one though; have you seen the price tags?

I was much more influenced by a couple of films I had seen called Mondo Enduro and Terra Circa. In those adventures they used much smaller Suzuki DR350. There are several advantages to this approach, primarily less cost to buy, lighter and better off road and they stand out much less to mark you out as a rich westerner to be taken advantage of. Budget wise it was always going to be a choice of second hand bikes and therefore subject to availability and popularity, hence price second hand. I was in favour of trying the Kawasaki KLE500. Although not thought of as a particularly 'adventure going' bike the prices were very keen at the time which would have afforded us a newer machine for the money. Also they have a relatively low seat height which would be very handy off road, and I thought that a twin cylinder engine would be much smoother over the long distances we planned to cover. We'll never know how that would have turned out because before I knew it, Al had gone out and bought a Yamaha XT600E. If there is one mantra everyone in the motorcycle overlanding community seemed to agree on it was that if you're going together, you should take the same bike. The logic is that there will be one set of problems to overcome, so learning will be easier, and one set of parts and tools to take. Also there will be no performance advantage for one rider, meaning that the other struggles to keep up. Therefore I had to go and buy one too.

To be fair it's not a bad choice, well tested for this sort of journey and highly recommended by several high profile motorcycle travellers. The first one I tried to buy didn't quite work out. The bike had no tax, so the seller volunteered to bring it to me in his van. After I'd agreed, I started having a few doubts. Rule one in my book of buying privately is to not buy anything which might be stolen. Still, I was ready to go ahead, but when he arrived I found that the registration document was not in his name. This was one alarm bell too far for me, and although he wasn't too happy I refused to part with the cash. I eventually bought one I found advertised on an auction site. It was particularly interesting as it had been already partly prepared for a long distance trip involving off road. I paid £1700 for the 5-6 year old bike, including the extras such as hand protectors, large capacity fuel tank, touring screen, 18" rear wheel, and even some hard luggage, albeit home-made style. The luggage was made up of a 'Metal Mule' brand frame but with panniers made from steel ammunition boxes. These were strong but heavy for a relatively small capacity, and tricky to open and close, but since a set of specially made luggage might cost the best part of the cost of the bike again I thought it was a bargain. One of my guiding thoughts at this stage was that the bike could easily be stolen when abroad and would be effectively uninsured, not only that but were it to have a major breakdown or other problem outside of Europe then any recovery would be uneconomical.

First thing first, to collect the bike I hoped would carry me to far flung places. Unfortunately it was in Hastings, 350 miles away and it was the middle of winter. Having recruited a friend to drive me down to Hastings we set off in icy conditions at around 4am. We reached the vendors house and the bike looked good in the flesh. At around lunchtime we set off back North. I'm forever indebted to Jon for driving a 700 mile round trip in bad conditions. Not to say that the 350 mile return leg on the bike was easy. At 70mph on the A1 around Yorkshire going through a patch of freezing fog, the bike suddenly lost power and would not maintain speed. I pulled over but then couldn't find anything wrong and the bike seemed to return to normal. After that for a while it seemed all was well. Unfortunately I'm no mechanic, and I wasn't to know that this was the first occurrence of a problem that would plague me for months to come.

I spent some time getting to know the bike, but that too didn't always go smoothly. It became clear over a practice camping trip and day to day riding that the bike was intermittently unreliable in the wet. Each time there was a problem I replaced or cleaned a different part trying to isolate the issue, hoping that at the very least the issue would be fixed by departure day.

Much as the bike was misbehaving, I did still check it for 'robustness'. Once, coming to a stop at damp downhill junction during a ride the front wheel locked under braking and I fell off landing hard on my right hip. Although I was quite badly bruised, the bike seemed to have crashed well with no damage, other than the odd scratch to add to the collection. In the interest of being thorough, I dropped it on the other side commuting one day when a car changed lanes and stopped in front of me as I filtered through traffic. This time the result was just a bent gear selector which was straightened out again easily at the roadside. Lots of time was spent experimenting with luggage layout to get the best weight distribution and comfort.

Then a major problem reared its head. My bike would not get an MOT certificate because some of the bolts which hold the exhaust to the engine had sheared off which allowed it to leak. It was very annoying because I would only need the MOT for a couple of months until I got out of the UK. The same applied for the tax I would have to buy, a full year's worth, even though I was leaving the country where anybody would know or care what the tax disc signified.

It wasn't the only mechanical issue. The bike's exhaust started smoking on start up. After researching the problem on the internet I thought I had identified what would fix the issue. The local Yamaha dealer agreed and I took the bike in for them to fix the problem of the clouds of blue smoke caused by burning oil whenever I started it up. For some reason, after failing to find a straightforward explanation of the symptoms on the web I doubted whether they would really be able to sort out of problem, despite their apparent confidence. When I got my bike back from the Yamaha dealer I found things were worse than I thought. They were useless. They didn't fix the problem, this became evident immediately on leaving the dealer on the bike when once again I was engulfed in smoke. The part they replaced as they believed it was the cause looked fine, no damage at all. On top of this the service was appalling. They carried out and charged me for an MOT, failing the bike on the three broken exhaust manifold bolts. I told them about the bolts at the start so if these were an MOT fail I felt they should have said so and not done any work at all! I became increasingly irate as nobody had bothered to let me know that the bike wasn't ready for me to pick up when it was supposed to be. As this was my lunch break from work it made me late returning, much to the displeasure of my boss. Riding the bike a short time later I discovered that it was now leaking oil onto my left foot as I rode along. It never did this before! Unfortunately even this level of shoddy workmanship didn't come as much of a surprise because when they had given the bike back to me the clutch no longer worked at all! After several aborted attempts to pull away I had to go back inside the dealer's workshop to get it sorted out. One of their mechanics had reassembled the pedal mechanism incorrectly. They also changed the brand new oil filter for no reason, overfilled the oil, and then charged me £150 for this "service"... which I argued down to £125. In summary, the work made no difference to the problem, cost more than I thought was fair and was not done on time. That was the end of any faith I might have had left in them. I booked the bike into another shop for the next day to see if they could do any better!

I got a completely different response to the bike from Armstrong Engineering, a local bike shop. Their place is of the old school, complete with zero customer comforts and a dangerously uneven workshop floor (for the mechanics to work on, but visible from the customer side of the counter). They just gave the bike a couple of advisory notices for the exhaust and the small number plate, so at last the bike had the vital MOT certificate. I decided not to bother getting the exhaust taken off as I just couldn't see it doing any harm. I went ahead and tried to seal it without going to the effort and expense of removing the engine and 'helicoiling' the bolts. I felt this was a victory over the unnecessarily picky and incompetent dealers. Although perhaps taking a machine around the world that had struggled so much with its MOT should have hit me as a bigger warning sign!

Al came to get his bike out of my garage one Saturday. He had been storing his bike and various boxes full of tools and other equipment there for a while. We reassembled the electrics and replaced a missing engine mount bolt. It didn't go off without drama though; on his way home the chain snapped. I had noticed that there were tight spots in it when I was oiling it earlier in the day, but didn't think it would break. Although I'm happy to say I did mention it before he rode it! Thankfully the AA recovered him. Not the most impressive start to a round the world trip, but better to get this sort of thing out of the way in advance. His Dad took the rest of his gear back in his car and my garage was once more my own.

I continued to commute on the bike, parking in the free spots in a multi storey car park near to work. The bike nearly filled all of the car park with oil smoke when I started it some nights. I worked out that if I left it on the centre stand rather than the side stand overnight then there would be no real smoke in the morning. I started leaving it on the centre stand during the day as well. That counts as a solution right?

One day the bike started pouring petrol out of the drain hole on the way home from work. I continued to use the bike as the problem stopped. It hadn't done it since the first instance. Another intermittent fault was all I wanted, so I ordered a new drain plug screw knowing that getting the old one out would be a nightmare as it was all rounded off. There seemed to be so many problems! I was fairly worried about the overall reliability of my bike, especially the oil burning issue. It was now doing it on every cold start and even if it turned out to be insignificant in the long term, at the very least it was fouling the spark plug, which is not good at all.

I tried to improve some other niggles on the bike too. I ordered new air and fuel filters and over the next week took the carburettor back off the bike with the intention to replace the rounded off drain screw. I was forced to give up though, because it was impossible to shift. So that turned out to be a waste of money for the new parts. I was also trying to get a good seal between the new air filters and the carburettor. This was another unnecessary problem caused by the tinkering of a previous owner. The original air box and standard air filter had been removed and replaced with cone shaped filters attached directly to the intake of the carburettor. These filters were not original parts and since they didn't have printed on them a size or model number it wasn't straightforward to order replacements. In retrospect I should have ordered them in a smaller size than I did, but it had seemed right when I measured them. In an attempt to make them fit I managed to fabricate some rubber tubes of the right diameter to make a connection between the new air filters and the carburettor. They were made from car inner tube, cut to size and glued together with jubilee clips at either end. I hoped that it would work, but looking back now it's hard to believe what I was thinking! The new air filters ended up being just plain too big. So I reinstalled the others with my new sealing system. I couldn't decide whether to try ordering some more or whether this would meet with just as little success! I had a similar dilemma as whether to order a new chain. I had a fear of making things worse rather than better and not having time to resolve the situation. In the end I ordered a new chain but decided to carry it as a spare for both bikes rather than fitting it from the outset. In the end I carried the heavy spare chain all the way to the end of my journey on the bike without it ever being needed, along with a load of other parts. This added to the feeling that I was prepared for lots of eventualities which never occurred but unprepared for lots of the ones that did!

I test fitted all my luggage and equipment to the bike so see how it would work. The tyres were awkward to carry and I was a bit worried that there wasn't enough room for everything. To be honest though I felt that if the visas came and the bike kept running everything else was not a big deal! I took my side stand to a welder to get a large footprint added. It took forever to find the place but when I got the side stand back from I found they had done a good job. This only cost me ten pounds but would stop the bike sinking into the ground and falling over on soft surfaces. This was one of the few modifications that actually worked and didn't cause any real problems. However, in reality the benefit was marginal and if going on a trip again I wouldn't bother. I had this feeling as departure approached that I didn't want to get into any major maintenance and repairs on the bike in case I broke something! Even at the time I knew this was probably a stupid attitude, but it was there. Soon enough it was time to do a final pack up of the bike. I went through the minor details like working out which credit cards to take. I also hid a spare key for the bike in the bike seat. This was a trade-off between a possible security risk and the risk of losing the first key and not being able to go anywhere!

I thought over whether I should take the tank back off and do another inspection and spark plug change. In the end I decided I would. I changed the spark plug and looked for any weak links in the ignition system, but everything looked fine. I reassured myself that all would be well. One of my last preparations was managing to get spare keys cut for my top box. Getting spare keys for unusual items such as this is sometimes easier said than done, but in the end my local shop was able to find an appropriate blank for minimal cost. I loaded the bike up pretty much completely. Other than final bits and pieces I felt that I was kind of ready to go.

Paperwork

A cross continental adventure such as ours can involve a lot of paperwork. Sometimes in modern Europe you could be forgiven for thinking that crossing any border is easy. Usually these days there is nothing but a small sign at the side of the road to indicate that you have crossed a border at all. However, for our chosen route many of the countries require a visa to be gained in advance from their embassy in London. This is not so convenient when you live three hundred miles away in Newcastle and several visas all taking some time to process and all with different rules about how far in advance they can be requested. Some applications are even more complicated and require extra paperwork such as letters of invitation. As a result we enlisted the help of two companies to help us with the process. Stantours provided us with some of the Letters of Invitation, and with the guided tour required for Turkmenistan. Travcour would co-ordinate getting our passports filled with all of the visas. This is a bespoke process for our individual route and timetable so still took considerable back and forth communication and a bewildering number of decisions. The first two visas to arrive were Kirgizstan and Uzbekistan. We gathered several letters of invitation via copies sent to us via email.

To get it out of the way I filled in the US immigration online visa waiver form required for UK residents. This was light relief really and easily done. I thought it much better to do it now though, than forget and arrive in the USA only to be turned back. Gradually paperwork arrived; the Turkmenistan letter of invitation was followed by the Tajikistan visa. Requirements for these countries are not always stable and in the middle of the process the letter of invitation requirements for Azerbaijan changed suddenly. The result was an extra cost of sixty pounds and a worry that it wouldn't get done in time.

Once the letter of invitation for Russia arrived I sent in my completed visa application. Normally a visa for Russia would have been more straightforward, but as we planned to enter into Russia twice a multi-entry business visa was required. This involved an invite from an imaginary Russian company. Quite what I would say if asked why two British "businessmen" would turn up at a remote border on dirt bikes I wasn't sure. While I did all this my passport was in the Azerbaijan embassy, but by mid- May we had all of the visas except the Russian one. I waited nervously for the passports to come back. They eventually did so, complete with visas, with just two days to spare before departure! I dutifully scanned all of the visa pages in to save an electronic copy, not that it would probably do us much good if we lost a passport!

Preparation

The hardest thing to do was decide to go. Many of the other preparations had a surreal sort of quality -; resigning was a particular case in point. The day after my thirtieth birthday, I resigned from my job as a Software Engineer working in the development team for a start-up company. There's no backing out after that point. Although the company was based in Guildford, the development team, all three of us, were housed in a small office in the centre of Newcastle-upon-Tyne. Resigning from my job was surprisingly difficult. I felt a loyalty to the people who had given me a chance and that it was very reckless to throw away a well-paid job especially since this was the beginning of what we all now know, as the Global Economic Crisis. I had to work as close as possible to the departure date to maximise the pot of cash available to fund this adventure. Stacking all of my furniture into the garage and putting the house on the rental market were just two of the things that were necessary to make the whole thing happen, although the house wouldn't actually be rented until I was thousands of miles away!

The day I resigned I decided to start keeping a log of the things that happened planning and having an overland adventure. It seemed like a good time to start. However, the real start of the process was many years ago when I started dreaming of having a long distance adventure on a motorbike. I've always loved cars and motorbikes as long as I can remember, and my love of travel has developed and intensified through my twenties. Keeping track of preparations might seem a bit over the top, but I wanted to try and get into the habit of writing often, so that I could write a reasonable log of the events which happen during the trip. I'm known among my friends and family for having a terrible memory. It's a great fear of mine that everything I do becomes a blur over time and I can't remember what happened from one year to the next. So I try to do things which will have such an impact that I cannot forget. This trip as a whole is certainly one of those, but I would still need help to remember the individual days. So I hoped that a log would supplement the photographs I would take on the way to jog my memory. My Dad wrote a brief log during his trip hitch-hiking to the Munich beer festival when he was a student. I thought it was a great record of the little details that would have been lost forever had he not written them down.

There were a few different motivations for going on an adventure of such magnitude. Firstly there are those that have gone before. There are hundreds of motorcycle travel books and web blogs that have been such an inspiration for this trip. They always make the places and people encountered sound so fantastical. A roller-coaster ride of ups and downs never to be forgotten and leaving the authors forever changed in some way. I felt that I was at something of a crossroads. Thirty years old, having worked in software since leaving university at twenty two, I'd never done the backpacking trip that many people do during or after university. At the time I'd been keen to get on with working, mainly to become independent by buying my own house, but also to feed my passion for all things automotive. I'd had my first driving lesson as soon as I could on my 17th birthday, and passed not long after. Motorcycle lessons were more of a challenge. My parents, like many are, were very against me riding motorbikes due to the risk of having an accident and being badly hurt. So I waited until I was working in my first "proper" job and began to take lessons in secret. While living with my parents and on the pretence of going out to see friends, I would go for a weekly lesson at a local motorcycle school on a nearby industrial estate. I passed my direct access test in due course, but getting a bike had to wait until I had moved out. Still, this was the groundwork for a motorcycling future I was yet to imagine.

There is a lot to think about getting ready for a trip like this. Not least of these was health. Taking the road less travelled requires a few more vaccinations than your average holiday. A few days after my birthday, I had had my first rabies injection. It really made my arm ache quite a bit, much worse than a normal flu jab. Two more are required at forty three pounds each, minus a ten percent discount at the Superdrug pharmacy for some reason! Tick Borne Encephalitis was another injection which I couldn't get courtesy of the National Health Service. Two are required when travelling and particularly camping, in areas which ticks are common. Certain ticks carry this disease which can be fatal if caught, especially if the nearest treatment is many days away. The injections unusually are taken one before the trip and one after, at sixty two pounds each. Expensive but better than being ill or worrying about it too much. It felt like trying to insure myself against the unknown. Even at the time I was pretty certain that the thing which ended up making me sick would be something I never thought of to begin with! Actually, it could be as simple as falling off the bike, which by this stage, as I've previously described, I'd managed to do twice already. On one occasion I had just been coming to a halt at a T-junction when a combination of downhill camber, damp greasy road and off road biased tyres meant I locked the front wheel, falling hard on my right hip. The bike was undamaged and I got away with a large purple bruise. Another time I was filtering through traffic on the way to work when a car tried to change lanes in front of me. However the traffic stopped forcing them to halt between lanes. I didn't break in time and hit the back of the car, breaking the rear light cluster. This time I didn't hurt myself but bent the bikes gear selector back. This was easily bent back into place. It was less easy to repair my damaged confidence! I brought the grand total of crashes in my riding career to three. The first being when I'd written off my first bike, the lovely black Suzuki SV650 I'd had from new.

I was still working and pretty busy at work right up until I left. The boss wanted loose ends tying up and projects finishing, so there was to be no quietly fading away allowed! They had my good will though; I always feel I should try to give my best even though my thoughts were elsewhere. I worked hard to finish up and keep on the good side of the boss, I was hoping that they might have a position available when I returned and wanted to make sure I'd be considered. Before resigning I had asked the company to consider allowing me a period of unpaid leave to go on the trip. However this was always a long shot in any company especially one so small. It was a shame but they turned down the request. By that stage I knew I was going to go regardless. I tried to look at the positive of the decision. At least I wouldn't have to worry about getting back within a certain time-scale to return to work. My girlfriend Helen was the only reason to come back other than running out of money or not enjoying the trip itself. I wasn't sure which would be the best reason to finish! I just had to hope that everything would come together for the best in the end. The days rolled on with bits and pieces of progress here and there. I got my second rabies injection and first Tick Borne Encephalitis injection. I also saw the dentist for a pre-trip check, which didn't throw up any problems.

I was training at the gym a quite a lot before the trip started. Not really for anything specific but the fitness and weight loss wouldn't do any harm. In my penultimate gym session I ran the 5000 metres in 19 minutes and 58 seconds. Now that I'm stopping training, it might be as fast as I ever get. I'm still pretty chuffed with that performance as I'd more or less given up trying to go faster since hitting twenty one minutes, but my general training seems to have worked to the extent where I knocked off half a minute without even trying, then bust a gut the very next day to break off the rest. I also lost about twenty two pounds in the process. OK, so I wasn't breaking any world records, but it wasn't bad for a fat lad with a beer habit! I had started about six months previously, with my girlfriend Helen's encouragement, going to the gym and being careful what I ate. I really like the feeling of doing positive things, and exercise is something positive you can do pretty much every day. There was little doubt I would lose the fitness again while away, but whether I gained weight or lost more seemed like it would depend on how the whole thing panned out.

When my final pay day before setting off came round, I bought some Euros and Dollars and ordered some bike parts online. I had a small Fujitsu Siemens GPS device which I had managed to re-program so that it would run TomTom 7 satellite navigation software. We were planning to use a Garmin device as these have much more mapping available for the less explored parts of the world. So I knew that in all probability the TomTom wouldn't be much use where we're going. However, as far as Turkey the TomTom had maps, so it might come in handy!

By early April I was falling behind with entries in the log already but was forging on with the little practicalities. I'd requested a phone unlock code, so that I could use other networks when abroad and checked with my bike insurer that I would be legally covered for riding through Europe, although I knew beyond that would be out of the question on a UK policy. Insurance would then be down to what could be bought on entry to each country, whatever that was worth!

Helen and I had been together 5 years. To celebrate we were going out for dinner when her car decided to celebrate by breaking down. Being a Rover, the head gasket had failed. We waited hours for the AA to come and rescue us. I tried not to take this as a bad omen but then I found out that my company, a hangover from an aborted period of IT contracting work between jobs, hasn't been struck off successfully. This was another thing I was dealing with prior to departure which added to the hassle. Eventually conversations with Companies House and the Inland Revenue seemed to sort everything out. I was just hoping it wouldn't cost more as a result, as when facing the unknown as I was, every penny seemed to count! As if to highlight this point I ordered a GB sticker (a legal requirement) online, refusing to pay what I felt was a crazy three pounds in the local Halfords store!

Much more significant and to the point, I ordered a new camera. I decided to go for a relatively inexpensive model, a Kodak Easyshare C913, which I figured would still be a big improvement on what I had already due to its 9.3 mega-pixel capability. Technology moves on so quickly that it probably would have been state of the art a few years earlier. I didn't think there was any point going for a top end model as it wouldn't make me a better photographer. I hoped that the subject matter and a bit of time spent on composition would more than make up for a lack of fancy features. Once the new camera arrived I happened to be looking at some photos from a holiday in Canada and the USA the previous year. The photos in good light were pretty decent, so I hoped the new camera could live up to and improve on the old one.

Scraping together money continued. I cashed in the premium bonds I owned having read that they were a worse bet than ever at the time. It was only two hundred and fifty pounds but I reasoned it might make all the difference at some point on the trip, so I cashed them in. I didn't stop there. I also sold all of my CD's and DVD's to a website online. This raised another £56 to the cause. I found this kind of thing quite therapeutic, the fewer possessions I had the better. I sold a motorcycle helmet that I had got for free from a magazine on an internet auction for fifty pounds, and a violin I'd never played for years. The guy who bought the violin was so pleased with his bargain I felt I'd given away a priceless treasure! It felt good to offset some expenses as time went along. Recently the car Helen and I shared cost £500 to fix which was a bit of a disaster and made me pretty broke alongside other recent expenses. I knew I would also end up owing money for shared items for use on the trip, as for some things there was no point taking duplicates. We also sold Helen's exercise strider. The money wouldn't be mine for the trip but it was another step forward to getting the house cleared ready for renting. To this day I consider having everything I own and need to survive strapped to a motorbike as pretty much the most free you can be. No ties and the power to move on your own schedule. Glorious!

I visited my doctor and got a prescription for some antibiotics and malaria tablets. The antibiotics I wanted were fairly general, to be used when all else had failed and there was no healthcare available. The doctor listened to what the plans were and empathised because he was planning his own travels in the future. This seemed to very much work in my favour as he even prescribed Malerone for me, a new malaria drug at the time, which meant just taking one tablet a day instead of several and has fewer side effects. Getting this and the antibiotics on the National Health Service meant I had to pay less than fifteen pounds prescription charge for the lot. After than it was just various over the counter medications that needed buying.

By mid-April I was feeling anxious, a bit worried about the trip. I wanted to make progress on all of the things written on my task list, but at the same time I was kind of reluctant to really grab the bull by the horns and get stuck in. I'm not sure what the problem was exactly. Partly I didn't want to upset Helen, as me talking about and working towards leaving seemed to do. It didn't make much sense as I was definitely going, but the actions towards it seemed to drive the reality home for her. It was flattering that she would miss me so much, but tough knowing something I was doing was hurting her. It was also somewhat surreal. I kept looking at the task list and not seeing anything I could immediately do, each task needing some other prerequisite before it could be completed. I needed to get going soon.

I was organising for my house to be rented out through a local agent, so they came to take photographs of the house for the website. I got the house cleared and all my furniture into storage so that the house could be advertised for rent without delay. It was strange to be flitting between Helen's parents' and my parents' homes, counting down to the big day. Somewhere in all this I forgot I had an appointment for a hepatitis-B injection. I got all the way to work, using the bus that day, and had to turn around and go back. I was too focussed on the estate agent coming to take photographs of the house.

Even dealing with utilities wasn't straightforward, leaving Sky television was more difficult than trying to leave the Mafia! The cancellation period was thirty one days, and then I still had to ring them back again to get the remainder of my money refunded. I had to wait a long time for my mobile phones unlock code from the provider. I was also in an 18 month contract for my land line and broadband connection, which would mean an exit penalty apparently. I also managed to sort out all of my online banking access, so I should be able to use accounts easily and transfer money while out on the road. Most daring stories of escaping the rat race don't mention this bit!

I ordered daily use contact lenses instead of my usual monthly versions. I thought that this would be better for avoiding infections when away from a nice clean bathroom to take lenses in and out. The downside was that they were fairly bulky and took up considerable space in one of my panniers. I had thought about having laser eye surgery so that I wouldn't have to deal with using contact lenses or glasses at all. However a combination of the cost and reading a number of horror stories of botched surgery encouraged me to just deal with contact lenses. The cheapest surgery was about £400 pounds per eye at the time, but even I had to concede that eye surgery wasn't an area I wanted to save money on!

Existing home life and trip preparation carried on side by side in a sort of uneasy truce. Helen and I went out for meals together and one weekend went for a break to a nearby Country House Hotel. I enjoyed it although it felt daft not to be fully concentrating on the trip. I forgot to take my new camera, it would have been a good opportunity to test it out We had been getting on well for the most part, despite the stress of the upcoming separation. At times, thinking of this would make Helen very upset. For my part, clearing out the house made me realise how ready I was for a change. Living in Dudley and working in IT might be safe, comfortable and easy, but it was also frustrating. More importantly it wasn't exciting or memorable, and that's what seemed most important to do before youth and opportunity slipped away. Even my friends' questions about the trip could make me annoyed as I didn't have all the answers! It felt like going through a separation also, dramatic though it may sound I couldn't be sure I would ever see them again.

At the time it was very exciting and I could see it was going to be pretty crazy seeing how things worked out. It seemed that literally anything could happen, from total breakdown while still in Europe, to making it all the way to the USA and beyond. I remember hoping that whatever happened I would come out of it better off in some way. I wanted to be more relaxed and confident, with wider horizons. Sometimes, even before the start, going on the trip seemed really stupid and like an expensive mistake, especially with a dodgy old bike. Other times I couldn't wait to get out there. All would depend on the bike really. I felt that if the engine would only hold together then everything would be OK. I hadn't checked the timing or the compression or the valve clearances or any of that stuff that maybe I should have. I just knew the thing was relatively safe because it got through the MOT no problem, barring noise. That didn't mean it wouldn't blow up though!

Each time I read more stories on other people's travels on the Horizons Unlimited Bulletin Board I couldn't believe we're going to try and do it myself. I wasn't at all sure I had a thick enough skin or an outgoing enough personality to survive it. My contracting experience had knocked my confidence a lot. I felt I had psychologically crumbled under the pressure. Mainly it was because I felt I wasn't up to the job, but there was a big element that I was away from home, Helen and my parents, whom I usually rely on for support and somewhere to vent my troubles. I just hope that anything which happens on the road doesn't feel like contracting did, because it was awful. I decided I would probably write a blog online, to let people at home know how things were going without updating everyone individually. However, on top of practical troubles about having the time to write it and not having a laptop to write it on as I went along, I knew that I would have to edit out the things that go wrong because those left at home would worry if they read it. So that's where this book fits in, the full story revealed in detail, warts and all.

By early May a lot had happened. I had finished work and did a few bits and pieces like filling in a tax return. I moved out over a weekend. This included managing to move the entire contents of the house into my separate garage for storage on the Saturday, and the majority of the cleaning on the Sunday, finishing on the bank holiday Monday. I got a lot of help from my parents and particularly my friend Jonathan, who brought his carpet cleaner and actually cleaned all the carpets for me. Place was a bit of a state when we started but looked pretty immaculate by the end, I could have happily moved back in! However, I dropped two sets of keys off with the estate agent and prayed for progress on letting the house as it would really help out with the finances. I still seemed to have loads to do and no time and panic was just beneath the surface! At least for now.

I almost didn't want to do the 'training run'. In my head I was thinking "If I don't instantly have a great time God knows what it'll be like doing it miles from home when I'm tired, lonely, hungry and scared." However the agreed weekend came around and I met up with Al at Scotch Corner services to take a cheesy photograph and begin our assault on the Yorkshire Dales. We wound our way from the A1 through Richmond and into the dales, stopping for the odd scenic shot. All went well at first and we checked out a couple of camping options before deciding on a spot behind the tea rooms at Hardraw where we set up our first camp.

It turned out that setting up was going to be considerably easier than the packing up, but we weren't to know that as we set off to see the local attraction of the Hardraw waterfall. It's nice in a waterfally kind of way, even if it isn't exactly Niagara. However it did serve the purpose of being our first experience of getting fleeced during our adventure biking travels by costing £2 to get in. This is because it is privately owned and "maintained". The best reason to stay in Hardraw is probably the Green Dragon pub since it is friendly enough, has a selection of real ales and the food is good. Not to mention an open fire, which being England you're not allowed to have your own version of in camp. Rules such as no camp fires are common place in the UK. Part of the attraction of this trip was to get far enough away from civilization that there was nobody left to enforce the rules. In fact, given that we wouldn't speak the language it was unlikely that we would even know what the rules were!

Overnight the gales and rain started, my tent just about stood up to it despite me not really putting it up properly. Al's fancy and massive 'biker' tent broke a pole on first use, but otherwise stood up OK too. We eventually got packed up in the bad weather and headed into Hawes for breakfast, which ended up being a decent full English at a cafe there.

Due to the weather we decided to cut short the riding and head for home. This was hardly an auspicious start with thousands of miles and many bad weather conditions looming! The drama wasn't over though, my bike decided to cut out due to getting a very wet HT lead. We got it going again with WD40 and as we got out of the rain it dried out and returned to normal running. Not exactly confidence inspiring, but I reasoned that at least we were heading south, so it should be dry right? It's not going to rain outside of England surely! Looking back over the memories of this it seems odd that I didn't replace the HT lead. I can only put it down to denial that the whole trip was really happening. Some mental issues there!

It was still mid-May when we had a family gathering and I struck lucky as I was given a tent, large Ortlieb dry bag plus pans and a petrol stove by my cousin, who had used them on various cycling trips all over the world in previous years. In the end I didn't end up taking the stove but I did use the tent on his advice, after realising it was probably superior to the one I had. It was in good condition considering the action it had seen. I sprayed it with a solution to re-waterproof it. I also began to spend a lot of time packing, trying different configurations to get the right balance of usability and weight distribution. I also bought a down sleeping bag after the experience of the training run. The new one was so much smaller and lighter than the old one that it had to be worth it, as long as it didn't get too cold! In the end I still think that even with all the attention on packing I took more things than were strictly necessary.

On the 21st of May I took the bike for a final test run and everything seemed OK. I filled with petrol, put some air in the tyres and checked the oil and brake fluid. I had an emotional goodbye with Helen at her parents, house. I told her I loved her and promised to come home to her. She was very conflicted between supporting me, and worrying that I would enjoy the freedom of the open road and wouldn't have a place for her in my life any more. My parents' next door neighbour popped round to the house and gave me chocolate and sweets to take which was a very nice gesture. A few people came over for farewell drinks before I left; nothing too big though. I'd had a few nice messages of support as well over the email. After all of the troubles I'd had with the reliability of my bike I remember my Dad asking if it was really up to the job of an ambitious journey like ours. I replied something like "It'll have to be" and pushed any negative thoughts to the back of my mind.

UK

On the morning of departure the bikes odometer read 10036 miles. The plan for today was to ride to a stopover point near Gatwick. I wheeled the bike out of my parents garage and set off alone to meet up with Al at the service station we had pre-arranged, which was an hour or so away. It would turn out to be a long day, riding over 350 miles. I was nervous setting off, but the ride was uneventful and I arrived at our rendezvous. When Al arrived his journey had not been so straightforward. He had already broken down on the way with an oil leak. This made me feel a little better about the doubts surrounding my own bike. Once we got going the miles slipped by, listening out for every squeak and rattle in a state of mild paranoia! By the time we joined the M25 to skirt around London the traffic had built up considerably. We had to split lanes in order to keep up any progress but with the aggressive commuter traffic and a heavily burdened bike feeling very wide, this felt like a gamble. My nerves were on edge until we left the hectic main roads and neared our destination.

However, there were no other major problems other than the petrol tank leaking petrol from the cap when accelerating out of slow corners. Al had organised for us to stay with some of his family, so it came as quite a surprise when he couldn't find the place. We had a few forays up the private driveways of various large private residences, each resulting in an awkward and precarious multiple point turn when it became clear that this wasn't the one. When we finally did find the right entrance, a quite lovely place revealed itself. It was a fairly large country house complete with grounds and a duck pond. We even had our own apartment to stay in, built separate from the main house above the large garage. The weather became better and better, turning into a beautiful summer's evening. There had only been a few spots of rain all day. I felt buoyed by the luxurious surroundings and generous hospitality.

France

The next day we got up full of optimism for another day filled with big mileage, hoping to get well into France. We had a hearty breakfast before leaving and I felt fully fortified by a good night's sleep. Not having to repack any of our equipment meant that getting on the road went so smoothly that we got an earlier train than planned from Folkestone through the channel tunnel. The sun was shining and the heat built steadily through the day, to the point where I couldn't believe how hot it was already! I had fitted a digital clock to the bike, as it only has basic instruments by default. The clock also had a built in thermometer, and on our very first day out of England, still only in May, it was showing the temperature at thirty two degrees Celsius! We were getting to grips with the various bits of technology we had with us as we went. So far the intercoms we had brought were not working and the Garmin satellite navigation seemed a bit hard to use as well. Being used to the ease of use and clear proprietary maps of TomTom, the Garmin seemed archaic. At least I had managed to play around with the mounting for my TomTom device so that I could see it properly. It was really a device designed for a car so the original mounting wouldn't have worked. The solution was a soft bag mounted from the windscreen. The Garmin system by contrast, was a bike specific model and had a lockable mounting bracket to place it conveniently on the handlebars. The final piece of satellite technology we had with us was a SPOT tracker. This device uses standard GPS to track your movement, but then also communicates with commercial satellites to plot the journey on a web page, so family can track your whereabouts. It also has the facility to send 'OK' messages to reassure them further. Finally, there was a function we hoped never to use, the SOS. As all these things happened via satellite rather than mobile phone network there would still be a way to communicate when there was no mobile signal. The bikes were running well so far, which was something of a relief. I had made a mental note to check the oil level every day, but for the second day in a row, I forgot. The highlight of the day was visiting the remains of the old Reims GP circuit. What used to be the track is a public road and it's strange to ride along and suddenly find crumbling old grandstands lining the road.

Reims-Gueux, as it was from 1926 to 1951, or just Reims from 1952 until it closure in 1972, was a triangular motor racing road course. Located, obviously, near Reims, France - it hosted fourteen French Grand Prix in its history. Reims-Gueux was first established in 1926 on the public roads between the small French villages of Thillois and Gueux. The circuit had two very long straights between the towns, and teams strove to maximize straight-line speed of their cars and during the racing many slipstream battles took place. Race organizers actually felled trees and demolished old houses in order to make the circuit even quicker.

Its first event was the Grand Prix de la Marne, staged in 1952 by the Automobile Club of Champagne. International racing came soon thereafter, with the first official Formula One event occurring in 1950, the inaugural year of the Formula One world championship. The circuit layout was shortened and changed in 1952 to bypass the town of Gueux, and the circuit was then renamed Reims. The layout was changed yet again in 1953, it was made slightly longer and faster; two fast curves and a hairpin further up the RN31 highway were added. The circuit was last used by Formula One in 1966 and the last car meeting was held in 1969. Motor bike racing continued for 3 more years and it closed permanently in 1972 due to financial difficulties. In 1997, there was to be a historic race held there, but for technical reasons, it was cancelled several months before it was due to take place and in 2002, the bulldozers arrived to demolish some portions of the track. Sections of the track around the pit lanes are still visible today.

The old RN31 straight between Muizon and Thillois has been widened and turned into a dual carriageway though it does follow the same line as the original 2 lane road that was raced on. It is still possible to drive a lap around the version of the circuit used until 1952 (though the old Garenne T-junction was obliterated as part of the widening of the RN31). It is no longer possible to complete a lap of the circuit used from

1953 onwards as the tarmac between Bretelle Nord and Muizon has been dug up. The annual historic meeting uses the Circuit d'Essais which came into being in 1952 and uses the 1953 circuit until La Hovette then turns onto the pre-1953 circuit up to Garenne. The lap record of the original circuit (1926–1951) was 2:27.8 by Juan Manuel Fangio in an Alfa Romeo 159, and the lap record for the faster circuit (1954–1972) was 2:11.3 by Lorenzo Bandini in a Ferrari. [i]

We stopped in the scorching sun to try and take in the atmosphere of the place. Through the heat shimmer it wasn't hard to imagine being part of a crowd watching the race cars of the day scream down the straight with the smells of hot engines and tortured tyres filling the air. As we continued on our way I couldn't help but feel nostalgic, thinking about a golden age which I wasn't part of and probably never existed, but somehow seemed far more exciting and romantic than the current day. Still, in some ways that's what this adventure was all about. To travel through time as well as space by going to places where progress hadn't had the same impact as it had in the first world. We had made a conscious decision to spend as little time as possible passing through Western Europe for a number of reasons. We would always be able to come back as it was so close to home, and we had both spent numerous holidays in Europe in the past. Not only that, but the developed world is expensive as a traveller, and going quickly now would give us more time and money to spend seeing as much as possible later on. Eventually, after riding about three hundred miles we arrived at a camp site at Brienne-le-Chateau. I managed to buy a few bottles of cold lager, which tasted like heaven after a hot day's riding. At the moment it still felt like a holiday and I hadn't yet made the psychological shift to take into account that I would be away from home for many months. The camp site was quiet, with only one or two other people staying. It was actually the second site we had tried as at the first there had been nobody there and unwelcoming barriers were set up across the entrance. Each individual pitch for camping was roughly separated from the next by ramshackle hedges made up of bushes and trees pruned over the years to give some privacy. Having set up the tents on grassy pitch opposite an area of tall trees planted in arrow straight rows I delved into the panniers and dug out some ration packs which I had generously been given by Helen's Sergeant Major Dad. They proved invaluable when, like today, we had not stopped to pick up any fresh food. Pre-packed food in a bag that you just heat up in a pan of hot water may not sound very appetising, but it tasted delicious. Washing them down with a glass of red wine made them even better, and helped restore good spirits, allaying any thoughts about how tough it was going to be travelling on these bikes, with their lumpy single cylinder engines, for day after day.

There were plenty of flying, biting insects at the camp site meaning that it wasn't too long before I retreated inside the protective mesh of my tent. However this was not before I had tried my 100% DEET anti-mosquito spray. I'd brought the strongest stuff I could find on the recommendation of other travellers. Then I made the mistake of getting it on my lips and in my eyes. I don't recommend this at all because it really burns and tastes disgusting! I'd turned my attention to getting my mobile phone to work. Due to the number of different countries I was going to pass through I had bought a 'global' SIM which promises cheaper texts and calls than a UK mobile 'roaming'. I managed to exchange texts that evening with Helen. The pain I was putting her through by embarking on this adventure weighed heavily and even though she was saying all the right, supportive words, I could tell she was missing me, which in a way was flattering. She's a tough cookie though and all I could really do was hope she would be OK. My mind wandered over the events of the day. So far I'd only spoken a grand total of two French words – 'Bonjour' and 'Merci' – to the attendant in one of those traditional petrol stations where your petrol is pumped for you. Another drawback of the choice of bike was making its presence felt. The seat was fairly hard and thin, meaning after many hours in the saddle my arse was chafing and sore. This was exacerbated by the very hot textile bike clothes I was wearing. I had valued waterproofness and crash protection over lightweight and ventilation, so it was no surprise that it was hot, but that didn't make it any more comfortable! It took quite some time to get used to the seat, and the first few weeks in particular saw me shifting around on the seat to try and get some relief from the aching. Overall I was enjoying it so far, but wasn't sure what months on end would be like. Everything was still friendly and familiar. We had met several groups of bikers over the course of the day, and all of them had given a Gallic wave of the left hand or a foot out for thank you or just to say "Hi". I wrote an entry into my diary lying on top of the sleeping bag in the evening warmth, and fell asleep.

The next day I was suffering from terrible hay fever and was cursing not having taken any anti-histamine before setting off. Riding along, nose itching, inside a helmet where it's difficult to scratch I'm pretty sure could be used as a form of torture. It wasn't long before I realised I had already ridden over a thousand miles from home. On leaving our first camping spot I'd checked the oil in the bike and found that all was well so far. That paved the way for an amazing morning carving through the countryside, really the kind of thing envisaged in my mind's eye before ever setting off. It wasn't the only cause for celebration, as we also got the intercom working. This seemed important for progress as we would be able to confirm navigation decisions and identify when to stop without having to pull over every time.

The low value of the pound against the Euro manifested itself in the expensive petrol prices. If there's one thing that you get used to on a trip like this it's buying petrol. Having a full tank of fuel always made me feel better, as if nothing could stop me again for a few hundred miles. We would have lunch at random cafés in the towns and villages we rode through, either early or late depending on what we came across and when. The heat had continued to soar; snippets of television in the café lunch stops told us that France had entered a major heat-wave unusual for the time of year. The thermometer told me the bare facts, 39 degrees Celsius showing on the gauge.

We had gained altitude to around three thousand feet, so it was cooler by the time we found another place to pitch our tents though, with a nice view of above the lapping waters of a large lake. This time we didn't have to rely on the ration packs I'd hauled from home, because we had stopped at the local supermarket for supplies. We tucked into sausages and burgers cooked on our petrol stove. Although I'd been eating healthily before the start, I seemed to have reverted to type already and pondered whether I would get fatter or thinner on this type of diet! I had plenty of time to think about it because getting to sleep on the steeply sloping ground of the camp site was something of a challenge! The layout of the camp site lent itself to pitching the tents a certain way around. Normally if there was any slope I would make sure to pitch my tent so that I would end up lying with my feet downhill and my head at the top. On this occasion I found that the slope was from the side and I spent all night slipping into the side of the tent and off my sleeping mat.

The rhythm of long days riding continued, sometimes for twelve hours. We pushed on, making as much progress as possible and not stopping until twilight. This could cause problems if a convenient place to camp didn't materialize at the right moment. By now we'd reached southern France and entered the Gorge du Tarn, a steep sided valley with a thin ribbon of tarmac draped along its edge. As we rode towards the famous Millau Viaduct this fantastic road twisted left and right, clinging to the cliff edge and sometimes disappearing into a tunnel before popping out into the sunlight once more. The road oriented tyres fitted to my bike gave good grip and I was thoroughly enjoying the experience when I heard a strange noise, a mixture of pinging and scraping. Then it was gone. Suddenly it was back again, only louder. It didn't take long to work out that the noise happened whenever I turned a corner. Time to pull over. On inspecting the bike the problem was immediately obvious, three of the four bolts holding the sump guard onto the frame had vibrated loose and bounced off down the road. The guard was now trailing on the floor causing the noise and lots of sparks! I dug around in the spares I had brought with me and found three bolts the right size to permanently fix the problem at side of road. Later on that day the heat guard covering the exhaust fell right off. The same problem had happened again. Then I discovered tell-tale white lubricant on both of the offending articles, a result of the disastrous work carried out pre trip by my local dealer. This lubricant was obviously doing its job rather too well and had been put where, particularly on a single cylinder bike like this, it would have been better to use thread lock. I hoped that there weren't any more surprises waiting undiscovered! The Millau Viaduct made a spectacular finale to the days riding and I tried to take a good photograph of what felt like the first major landmark on my mental road map of the route. The poppies were blooming in the field where we had stopped at the side of the road to get a decent view. They made a pretty foreground with the graceful white legs of the viaduct rising from behind them towards the blue sky.

The Millau Viaduct is a cable-stayed bridge that spans the valley of the River Tarn near Millau in southern France. Designed by the French structural engineer Michel Virlogeux and British architect Norman Foster, it is the tallest bridge in the world with one mast's summit at 343.0 metres (1,125 ft) above the base of the structure. It is the 12th highest bridge deck in the world, being 270 metres (890 ft) between the road deck and the ground below. Millau Viaduct is part of the A75-A71 autoroute axis from Paris to Montpellier and the construction cost was approximately four hundred million Euros. It was formally inaugurated on 14 December 2004, and opened to traffic on 16 December. The bridge has been consistently ranked as one of the great engineering achievements of all time.[ii]

Communication with home was already patchy and a cause for concern, but I did find out that our SPOT tracker system was a big hit, with several people commenting that they were following my progress on a daily basis at home. Things weren't all rosy. Although it was still early in the journey I was worried about the relentless pace we had to keep up to cover the distances we had set ourselves on time. It was physically taking its toll now with Al complaining of back pain. Other niggles compounded the physical effort: the laptop Al had brought, and I was relying on also, had died, a victim of the constant vibration from his bike. The prospect of a morale boosting night in floating luxury on a friend of Al's motor launch evaporated as the news came through that it had broken down. At least it wasn't just us that had mechanical issues (my hand were already impregnated with engine oil from various mishaps), but I remember still feeling very unsure of how far we would get. There was never too long to dwell on any doubts though, the effort of each day meant that sleep came quickly and the prospect of Italy loomed large ahead.

However enjoyable all the twisting, turning roads were, they were also time consuming. We tried to leave the twisty stuff behind and stick to faster roads for a while up until we neared the Col du Turini. The road through the gorge leading up to it was an amazing, sweeping fast 'A' road which went on for miles. I had heard of the Col du Turini in the UK, as a legendary driving road. My first visit to the Alps was really making a big impression, however when we at last got to the Col itself we found it closed. The Col de Turini at its highest point is 1607 metres above sea level. It is a high mountain pass in the Alps in the department of Alpes-Maritimes in France and it lies near Sospel, between the communes of Moulinet and La Bollène-Vésubie near Nice which sits on the southern coastline of France west of Monaco. It is famous for a stage of the Monte Carlo Rally which is held on the tight road with its many hairpin turns. Until a few years ago, the Col de Turini was also driven at night, with thousands of fans watching the "night of the long knives" as it was called, due to the strong high beam lights cutting through the night. I suspect that this might also be a reference to the number of drivers who have come to grief driving here at race speeds at night. It is treacherous enough during the day! The Col de Turini has also featured three times in the Tour de France (1948, 1950 and 1975) and averages 7.2% gradient over its 15.3 kilometre length when approached from the East starting at the valley of the river Vésubie. This pass was featured in the first episode of Top Gear series 10 when the presenters went in search of the greatest driving road in the world.[iii] In fact this was probably where we had first heard about it.

Disappointed that the pass was closed, we nevertheless pushed on. Up and down many similar roads full of switch back turns and lethal looking drops, we balanced our biking enthusiasm for speed with the knowledge of the danger and a keen appreciation that crashing in France, our first foreign country, would not bode well for the next dozen or more to come. It was particularly windy making these roads even more scary than usual. The roller-coaster came to an abrupt end at Monaco. We rode some of the Grand Prix circuit and took photographs at the marina where workers were all busy setting up grandstands and banners for the Grand Prix to be held the following weekend. We didn't stay long in Monte Carlo as it is not the sort of place for scruffy travellers on a budget, and left on the first toll road we had used on our journey so far. It was so much faster than the coast road we had used to get there. Somehow I accidentally failed to pay, as I couldn't get the automatic barrier to work. Eventually it lifted regardless and I slipped through hoping that the local police hadn't caught the incident on camera and would come chasing after me! We had pulled into a motorway service station for a break. As the darkness gathered and we went to leave, I found that my bike wouldn't start. The thought of being stuck in the dark in a noisy service station as it got later, and we got more and more tired was unappealing to say the least. There was no sound at all from the starter motor so the problem was clearly electrical. A bit of fault finding later and the fault was traced to a dirty earth connection to the battery. Having cleaned it up the bike burst into life once more. We rode on, passing the simple sign denoting the border with Italy. At the second time of asking, we found a camp site that could squeeze us in. This place was rammed full of mobile homes and caravans with their ageing owners pottering around outside. I really couldn't see the attraction in coming to stay here on holiday, there wasn't so much as a view to enjoy! Still, I discovered that the place wasn't all bad. There was a bar, allowing me to finish the day with cold beer and Barcelona 2 Manchester United 0 live on the television. Afterwards I called Helen for one of her much needed pep talks ('pep' was something she regularly has in abundance!) and drifted off to sleep anticipating a better look at Italy over the coming days.

Italy

With the odometer clicking around to over one thousand seven hundred miles since home we took the toll Autostrada towards Como. It was a more expensive way of travelling but much faster and simpler to navigate. It was frustrating though to hit long queues at the toll booths, after all we were paying extra for the privilege of speed. I soon noticed that local bikers were filtering through the queue between the lines of cars and pushing in at the front. It looked pretty cheeky to my British sensibilities to queue jump like that, but it looked like it was the done thing here. Deciding that when in Rome we should do as the Romans do, I squeezed my bike to the front of the queue being careful to avoid eye contact with any of the car drivers. To be honest though, nobody seemed to mind.

Sometime previously the rubber strap which held in place my bike's battery had snapped and that in turn had caused the accessory circuit in the electrics to fail. I got it fixed without too much trouble later, but for now it meant no TomTom to help navigate. The device I was using was now several years old. The battery in the navigation unit itself was very poor and would run flat in minutes without a constant supply of 'mains' power. We found ourselves arriving at our chosen overnight stop at Lake Como quite early in the day, although just late enough for the nearest shop to have shut for the day. The camp site we had chosen was very close to the Lake Como shoreline. We walked down to the water's edge where a wide footpath ran along the side of the lake. Taking a seat on a park style bench we set up our petrol stove and cooked our boil in the bag dinner while watching people stroll by, walking their dogs or heading home, and just taking in the view. This was not at all unpleasant with a bottle of wine, which was rapidly becoming our custom! Being such a popular tourist area the roads were very busy. Our large overburdened motorcycles seemed ungainly compared to the scooters which zipped around overtaking us on either side. It seemed like only a matter of time until one of the scooters, and their rider, was unceremoniously squashed under a car or truck. I tried to catch up on the little maintenance tasks that had started to build. The clutch on the bike needed adjusting and the oil topping up. I addressed some problems with my bike trousers too, sewing the knee armour firmly into place as I always got my foot caught while putting them on and tore away the Velcro which was supposed to hold them in. I'd finally worked out that I'd have to turn my bike trousers inside out to dry them each evening. It sounds pretty disgusting, but the fact is that the linings were soaked with sweat from wearing then all day in the heat. The trousers being wet also encouraged friction sores to develop on my legs. While I had the needle and thread handy I repaired a hole which had developed in my front panniers. One side had been slightly overstretched by the petrol can held inside for extra fuel range, and the stitching came away. With the pleasant weather and pretty surroundings I was starting to warm to Italy after being strangely sad to leave France behind.

After Como, there was more motorway as we continued our path east. This constant riding at higher speed seemed to have a bad effect on me due to the jack-hammer type vibrations coming through the handlebars. By evening I could hardly hold a pen to write an entry in my diary. My right hand was more badly affected than my left as it's the one you use to hold the throttle open. With my left hand I could take it off the handlebars for a rest when I wasn't changing gear. Also there was no need to grip as firmly with the left hand during riding. My thumb on my throttle hand was agonizingly painful and my fingers refused to unfurl from the grip shape they'd been forming all day.

In other ways though, the journey had become spectacular. The Stelvio pass had been a noted landmark on the route from the beginning. It had been proclaimed by the motoring press as one of the greatest driving roads in the world. We were happily slicing up the mountain side, admiring the views as we gained height and stopping regularly to take photographs. Al decided that we had missed a must have shot, a short way back down the road and that we should get the bikes into the frame. In my heart I knew that turning my heavy bike around on the steep and heavily cambered road was a mistake, but not wanting to complain I started the manoeuvre. Sure enough, I overbalanced and fell to the ground dropping the bike. I wasn't hurt, and dropping the bike at such a low speed surely wouldn't have caused any problem. However, upon getting the bike upright again all wasn't well. The engine would restart and run, but the bike wouldn't go into gear. We stared at the bike in disbelief, unable to see anything wrong with it from the outside. We stood thinking of options and throwing around ideas of how to solve the issue. After a while a plan formed. Thankfully I had noticed a sign with a motorcycle on it in the last town we had passed through before starting to climb up the Stelvio. It looked like it should belong to a workshop, and if they were open maybe they could fix it. I just had to get the bike there. In neutral and with the engine off I pointed the bike back down the slope and began to roll. On the steep ground I picked up speed quickly, but had to slow down for the hairpin bends. Throwing caution to the wind I tried to keep as much speed as possible, so that when the ground levelled out towards the bottom of the pass I would still have enough momentum to make it down. Incredibly, I rolled all the way to potential salvation at "Bobomoto", to whom the motorcycle sign had belonged, without having to push more than a few yards. It wasn't over though, as being in continental Europe, everyone was on an extended lunch break and there was nothing to do but sit and wait. I gradually got burnt in the midday sun as the minutes ticked away. Al rang a contact at home to ask for mechanical advice, and received the gloomy prediction that the gearbox could be broken. I couldn't believe this could be true though, having dropped the bike so gently and virtually at a standstill. Eventually there were signs of life from the garage and using lots of gestures I managed to get across what the problem was to the guy who seemed to be the head mechanic, and maybe the owner.

Leaving his planned work to deal with us first, he found the problem in seconds. Cue embarrassment at our lack of mechanical problem solving skills! The issue was simply that the front cog which drives the chain to the back wheel had become dislodged. The nut holding the cog in place had obviously worked its way loose and dropped off, either when I dropped the bike or in fact, at any time previously! The garage didn't have a replacement nut to fit, but without a word of shared language my new favourite mechanic found a slightly undersized nut and clamped it into a spinning lathe type machine. He proceeded to expertly rethread the nut to the correct size. It fit perfectly, but since it had already become loose once might do so again. The mechanic indicated that he could weld it into place, and I nodded my approval. If it ever needed removing we would cross that bridge when we came to it! I'd read of people doing this under similar circumstances on the internet and the two little spot welds he added didn't look like they would be too hard to grind back in future. The bill was fifty Euros and I was so happy to be back on the road without further trouble or delay I paid up with a smile on my face. The location of the place with only gravity to get there had been so lucky!

We charged back up the mountain more quickly the second time around, as we'd done the photos the first time!

On reaching the top of the pass we rolled through snow fields in noticeably colder temperatures before heading down the equally twisty road on the other side. We moved as quickly as possible to make up the time lost getting the repair at Bobomoto, and barring a minor re-occurrence of an electrical gremlin there were no further dramas. When we finally rolled into a camp site I was relieved to see a restaurant attached. This would save cooking, and enough beers to generate a hangover the next morning were well deserved after such an eventful day. The camp site was on a lake near the town of Trento. We had developed the habit of heading towards lakes to find a camp site, as they were often common there and had good views. The view wasn't so memorable here, but the food was. This was our first meal at a restaurant during the journey. Being Italy it would have been rude not to try a pizza. It tasted incredible; I can honestly say I've never had one as good since. Whether it was and time and place, or whether the fresh ingredients and local expertise were genuinely that good, I may never know.

Slovenia

By the end of the day my diary read: Day 8 – 30/5/09 – Croatia's Adriatic Coast – 2200+ miles in!

Two thousand two hundred miles covered and the bike hardly broke down at all today! It's a bit of a worry that this should come as such a cause of celebration. And it is a lie, there was a brief re-occurrence of the electrical earth problem, but that hardly counts right? We skipped across the rest of Italy on the toll roads in as short a time as we could. Before leaving, Al bought a replacement laptop from a large out of town electrical store. There was no border control to speak of so we rode straight into and through the corner of Slovenia. Slovenia looks lush and green and worth exploring, but our perception of needing to keep going and keep to time meant that we had to cut our intended stay in the country very short indeed. There was just a quick check of our passports and we were into Croatia. In Croatia the scenery was stunning; the coast road was spectacular and a pleasure to ride along. Nevertheless I couldn't help but think we were doing too much, I was tired and concerned about the bike. I wasn't feeling at my most positive, with yesterday's sunburn reminding me it was there by itching annoyingly. On the good side though, I borrowed Al's cruise control which seemed to help my hand to recover. The cruise control is a moulded plastic device which clips to the throttle twist grip and allows the rider to keep the throttle held open just using the palm of their hand rather than having to keep a firm grip. It was impossible to believe that I'd only been away from home a week as such a lot seemed to have happened. The lack of time and internet access was a particular pain, making me feel rushed and under-planned as well as not being able to update family at home. Even phone calls were super expensive now that we were out of the European Union. We had no local currency so it was either Euros or a credit card, but it didn't cause a major problem.

Lightning stuck a second time in Croatia. The new laptop Al had bought the very same day back in Italy refused to work. I managed not to say that it would have been a good idea to see the laptop working in the shop before buying it, as I don't think that retrospective advice would have gone down too well! The laptop put Al in a very bad mood (in hindsight this bad mood was a warning sign to the epic tantrums that were to follow on the trip) and he went off for a walk on the beach. I was starving hungry, and after waiting for a while went off to check that he hadn't thrown himself into the sea. I really believed that was a possibility as Al's moods already seemed erratic, either very up or very down compared to my more placid demeanour. I'm sometimes accused of being too laid back. I wasn't expecting things to be this hard so soon, and neither of us were coping that brilliantly. I felt almost like I never took the reliability of the bike seriously before the trip and tried to snap out of negative thoughts before they started making me depressed! My golden rules of foreign travel were to stay out of prison and stay out of hospital. We were managing that so far, so how bad could things really be?! Good points noted in my diary were

1. The Weather

2. No Accidents

3. Bike still going

Croatia/Bosnia

In fact, I kept the bike topped up with oil and it didn't cause any further problems as we continued down through Croatia. We continued on the coast road for a while, and then switched to a toll road to save time. After that it was the coast road all the way to just past Dubrovnik and our camp site. Dubrovnik is a Croatian city on the Adriatic Sea, in the region of Dalmatia. It is one of the most prominent tourist destinations in the Mediterranean, a seaport and the centre of Dubrovnik-Neretva County. Its total population is about forty five thousand and in 1979, the city of Dubrovnik joined the UNESCO list of World Heritage Sites. The prosperity of the city of Dubrovnik was historically based on maritime trade. As the capital of the Republic of Ragusa, a maritime republic, the city achieved a high level of development, particularly during the 15th and 16th centuries. Dubrovnik became notable for its wealth and skilled diplomacy. The beginning of tourism in Dubrovnik is associated with the construction of the Hotel Imperial in Dubrovnik in 1897. Dubrovnik is among the best preserved medieval walled cities in the world. Although Dubrovnik was demilitarised in the 1970s to protect it from war, in 1991, after the breakup of Yugoslavia, it was besieged by the Yugoslav People's Army (JNA) for seven months and received significant shelling damage.[iv] With our hurrying along, not only had we by-passed Dubrovnik, only seeing it from a distance, but we had also missed out the Mostar Bridge in Bosnia, famously re-built after it was destroyed in the Balkan conflict.

The Mostar Bridge is known locally as Stari Most which in English just means 'Old Bridge'. It is now a reconstruction of a 16th-century Ottoman bridge in the city of Mostar in Bosnia and Herzegovina that crosses the river Neretva and connects two parts of the city. The Old Bridge stood for four hundred and twenty seven years, until it was destroyed on 9 November 1993 by Croat forces during the Croat–

Bosniak War. Subsequently, a project was set in motion to reconstruct it, and the rebuilt bridge opened on 23 July 2004. One of the country's most recognizable landmarks, it is also considered one of the most exemplary pieces of Islamic architecture in the Balkans and was designed by Mimar Hayruddin, a student and apprentice of the famous architect Mimar Sinan.[v]

Add to the list of missed stops the Durmitor National Park. The Durmitor National Park, created in 1952, includes the massif of Durmitor, the canyons of Tara, Sušica and Draga rivers and the higher part of the canyon plateau Komarnica, covering the area of 390 km². It was inscribed on the list of UNESCO World Heritage Sites in 1980. Eighty kilometres long and one thousand three hundred meters deep, the Tara River Canyon in the Durmitor National Park is one of the largest in the world.[vi]

Missing these stops was all in the name of getting a day ahead of schedule, to give more flexibility later on. I justified these in my mind, thinking that we were still only a short flight from home so could come back some day; it still seemed a shame though. Al's moods continued to fluctuate, getting better but then weird again in a matter of hours, and here's me thinking it was just the women in my life that were moody! I reasoned that unless you come away on an adventure like this all by yourself then you have to make compromises. What was difficult was that I felt that the bad moods were being taken out on me personally, like they were always my fault. I began to wish that we had not agreed to share so much kit. Having absolutely everything I needed to continue alone would have had its own advantages. Maybe we could have taken a few days off from each other by going a different route. At the very least it would have made me more confident of my independence and not so afraid to speak my mind in case of causing conflict. All I could do was stay quiet. Al's bike showed a few signs of mechanical trouble itself at one point, but then seemed to clear up again on its own. At our stopover for the night I chatted to another biker who was also touring in the region. We ate in restaurant near our Dubrovnik camp site where they served us a huge shared meat platter. It was excellent with succulent cuts of meat and tasty sausages. The feast provided a most welcome boost to morale and my energy levels.

Montenegro/Albania

The border crossing to Montenegro was the first place where they insisted that we bought insurance, refusing to accept that we were legal with our existing cover. On our itinerary the highlight was supposed to be Kotor Fjord, but the rain and mist spoiled the view and made it look like nothing special. The Bay of Kotor, known locally simply as Boka, is a winding bay of the Adriatic Sea in south-western Montenegro. The bay, once called Europe's southernmost fjord, is in fact a 'ria' or coastal inlet of the disintegrated Bokelj River which used to run from the high mountain plateaus of Orjen. The bay is about twenty eight kilometres long from the open sea to the harbour of the city of Kotor. It is surrounded by mountains of Orjen on the west and Lovćen on the east. The narrowest section, Verige strait, is only three hundred metres long. Despite that it has a shoreline of over a hundred kilometres in length. As of 2013, it can be crossed by a ferry boat, but Montenegro is planning to build a bridge to span the strait, the so-called Verige Bridge. The bay has been inhabited since antiquity. It's well preserved medieval towns of Kotor, Risan, Tivat, Perast, Prčanj and Herceg Novi, along with their natural surroundings, are major tourist attractions. The natural, cultural and historical region of Kotor has been a World Heritage Site since 1979. The religious heritage of the land around the bay — it's numerous Orthodox and Catholic Christian churches and monasteries — makes it one of the major pilgrimage sites of the region.[vii]

The "main" road, which was actually nothing more than a city street, was being dug up and we had to squeeze past vans and cars coming the other way, while trying not to fall into a trench. This meant slow going. Once away from the towns the road to the border was a bumpy single track affair that gave the impression that not many people came this way. The border guard wished me good luck leaving Montenegro. I'm not exactly sure what he meant, but it had the effect of making me pretty apprehensive on entering Albania. Albania is one of the poorest countries in Europe and just by looking at it was clearly the poorest country we had been to yet. The area just on the Albanian side of the border I could only describe as a dump. It was very untidy with rubbish strewn everywhere. Riding away from the border the roads gradually improved but the driving manners did not. This was the first time I felt the driving standards of the country we were in were really dangerous. Although the road was quite wide it was still only a single lane in each direction. The local nut-cases would overtake head on towards each other regardless of what was coming the other way, creating a four lane maelstrom reminiscent of Wacky Races. I didn't want to go out in a cartoon ball of flames or hit a car head on and fly through the air in a comedy style!

The only new and flashy things I saw in Albania were the petrol stations. These were placed literally every two minutes travel on both sides of the road and looked brand new and immaculate. This contrasted with the many dead cats and dogs lying forlorn at the side of the road, having lost their battle with the traffic. The other common sight was police speed traps, so we continued with caution not wanting to give an excuse for the police to pull us over. Being foreign and motorcyclists already made us prime targets. Not all attention was bad though, in fact far from it. The kids here all seem to love bikes and they were always smiling and waving. When I had a free hand from controlling the bike and avoiding accidents I would wave back. That would raise smiles and cause them to throw thumbs up signs in our direction.

Something big was happening in Tirana, maybe election or EU membership I wasn't sure. Tirana is the capital and largest city of Albania. Modern Tirana was founded as an Ottoman town in 1614 by Sulejman Bargjini, a local ruler from Mullet (business up front, party in the back!). Tirana became Albania's capital city in 1920 and has a population of over three hundred thousand; including the suburbs Tirana has more than four hundred thousand inhabitants.[viii] The traffic here was crazy and there were streets closed off with people everywhere, corralled by numerous police. I could feel the intense heat radiating from the air cooled engine beneath me as we were crawling through the city centre. Al seemed panicked as the road closures had confused his Garmin navigation device, so I took the lead and fought my way through the swell of people and cars. Using nothing more than a rough sense of direction and some luck the streets eventually deposited us out of the other side of the city. It started to rain making our surroundings look more grey and dismal than they probably were. Although I managed to struggle through the first bank of rain, the bike clearly wasn't happy in wet conditions and a second downpour encouraged us to take cover in a hotel. It seemed like good value at twenty five Euros for the night. Safe inside the basic hotel, our attention could turn to communications and technology. Picture messaging was supposed to be cheaper than a standard text to reach home in many countries, but they refused to send so there was no advantage to be had. I still had no internet access either so felt pretty cut off. All I had for company was all of the insect bites I had managed to pick up. There were some on my back and arm that were particularly swollen and an even more irritating one on my face!

Greece

Waking up in Albania, we tentatively explored the hotel to find breakfast. I ended up with a very dodgy omelette filled with mysterious unnamed "white cheese", but the coffee was good and both were included with the price of the hotel which was great. Hitting the road out of Albania, the surface improved and even the speed traps seemed friendlier as the police would sometimes wave or salute as we passed. There was a charge of two Euros each to leave Albania, not that I could work out what on earth this might be for. Still as it was dwarfed by the fifty Euros green card charge necessary to get into Macedonia it hardly seemed to matter. The border guard wasn't taking no for an answer on this issue. It was pay up or be sent back. There were pleasant landscape scenes and road conditions in Macedonia. Along the way we met Bert, a German biker on Yamaha MT-01. Other than the odd word he was the first fellow biking traveller we got to speak to on the journey. Although his road oriented machine was much more powerful and faster than our bikes he had no real tread left on his rear tyre. As a result he was nervous that it would burst, leaving him stranded. As a result he rode along with us all the way through Macedonia and into Greece as far as Thessaloniki, where he hoped to find a replacement. The exit from Macedonia was slow but in contrast the Greek officials cheerily waved us in once they realised we were British and German rather than Albanian. The road through Greece was very good fun with panoramic views of the countryside. It was good to be 'back in civilization' after what had seemed quite a different feel, particularly in Albania.

We rode an extra-long stint through Thessaloniki and onwards on the motorway to get us to the coast. On arriving at the first town which had the feel of a beach resort we asked at a bar if they knew of a camp site. There was a bit of a language barrier, but the helpful bartender called an English speaking girl who pointed to the camp site down the road. She wasn't sure if it would be open, but despite her concern, it was. We rode all the way down onto the beach and took pictures of ourselves and the bikes on the sand.

It felt like a good achievement at the end of the day to have made it to the southern edge of Europe. The camp site turned out to be a nice informal place, even if it was replete with copious insects, which proceeded to repeatedly bite me on the head while I erected my tent. We beat a hasty retreat and walked a mile or so along the beach to the area where the town's bars met the sea. It had a real holiday feel, although it was a place where Greek people came for their vacation rather than an invasion of Brits. I drank four beers and each one was delivered with a free bottle of water. They were taking hydration very seriously here! Over the course of the evening we had a couple of trips to a local style take-away where I introduced Al to the joys of Gyros, being as I was a veteran of the common Greek fast foods due to past holidays in the Greek islands. Tired but happy this felt like enjoying a final taste of the good life before the anticipated hardships in the 'Stans'. The only fly in the ointment was that Al lost his intercom radio on the final motorway section before arriving. Dropping at speed, it could be anywhere and had probably smashed into a thousand pieces. This rendered our expensive communications set useless, so from now on we would have to stop at the side of the road to speak. At some point later I decided my equipment was now just dead weight and reluctantly threw it in a bin.

Turkey

As we pushed onwards to leave Greece behind the landscape was barren and the weather very windy. At some points it felt as though I had to lean the bike over to forty five degrees just to keep going in a straight line. Despite this, progress was good thanks to the good roads. The Turkish border was the most intimidating to date, with large austere buildings and plenty of armed guards. We arrived in the early afternoon and it was difficult to know what the process was. Without any English signs or obvious queuing system, it was a case of trial and error. We managed to buy a visa OK, costing fifteen Euros. We weren't done there though; just as we thought all the paperwork was complete and we arrived at the final gate, with Turkey spread before us, we were sent back for insurance. It turned out to be only two Euros per person though. That finally did it and the guard let us through. We continued to ride on for a while, getting away from the border area, and found a camp site about eighty miles from Istanbul. My bike was running well, but I still reminded myself to keep checking the oil level and every nut and bolt I could find for tightness. Although it was currently dry in the back of my mind I wanted to try and make the bike more weather proof. To this end I wrapped as much of the electrical system as possible in plastic to try and protect it. Our camp site was almost on the beach. Quite a find really after the only other option, which despite looking like a huge and very orderly camp site from a distance, turned out to be a camp for construction workers busy with a nearby project.

Lying in my tent I could hear the waves lapping against the sandy beach and rock pools beyond. Although this place was very basic, and still going through the motions of being readied for a new season, it did have wireless internet. The signal didn't reach to the tents so I sat with my phone near the little building from where the signal seemed to be coming. This was the first access I had gained so I used it to check my email. I tried to make an entry to my online blog also, but was met with an error message, so it wasn't to be. It had been pretty hot that day, over thirty degrees Celsius. It was clear from the border that we were leaving the familiarity of the European community for good, and Al seemed nervous about it, unsure of the surroundings. I felt OK but certainly not as relaxed as I had felt the night before in the friendly atmosphere of the Greek beach resort. Although I'd thought that this camp site was more or less deserted, gradually the other residents began to make themselves known. Lines of ant and other creepy crawlies scurrying through the course grass made me feel like I was getting thoroughly bitten. I heard from home that Helen had set off on a trip to Malaga. She'd planned a whole summer of activities with her friends to keep herself busy while I was away, and it sounded like it would be somewhat more glamorous and a lot more comfortable than my current surroundings!

Diary reads: Day 13 – 4/6/13 About 2500 miles – Arrive Istanbul

Istanbul is Turkey's most populous city as well as its cultural and financial hub. Located on both sides of the Bosphorus, the narrow strait between the Black Sea and the Marmara Sea, Istanbul bridges Asia and Europe both physically and culturally. Istanbul's population is estimated to be between twelve and nineteen million people, making it one of the largest cities in Europe and the world. [ix]

On the morning of our thirteenth day travelling East Al's laptop seemed to magically come to life and connected to the camp wireless internet. We used this to find a hostel in Istanbul. Accommodation, particularly the type we could afford was centred on the Sultanamet area of the city. This was very useful, because it gave us somewhere to aim at, and we knew that as long as we could find it there would be no issue with it being fully booked. Istanbul is massive, the ugly outskirts were strewn with tower blocks and the traffic was extremely heavy. As if knowing that it was coming to the end of its maps, and therefore its capabilities, TomTom played its party piece, taking us perfectly around the maze of one way streets to the door of the hostel. Ironically, I found that satellite navigation was much more of a godsend here, in a big city with heavy traffic, despite all the road signs, than it would become in the huge expanses of Mongolia. On arriving, we locked the bikes to a tree growing up through the footpath, and noted that there was another motorbike parked nearby. The white and yellow Suzuki DR350 was scruffy looking like ours, and British registered. The private twin room we had booked somehow became places in a dormitory by the time we arrived. However on checking it there was no evidence of anyone else in the room. I was happy to be in Istanbul, and very pleased with the location of the hostel as it was right next to the famous Blue Mosque. The Sultan Ahmed Mosque is a very historic mosque in Istanbul. The mosque is popularly known as the Blue Mosque for the blue tiles adorning the walls of its interior. It was built from 1609 to 1616, during the rule of Ahmed I. Its Külliye contains a tomb of the founder, a madrasah and a hospice. The Sultan Ahmed Mosque is still popularly used as a mosque.[x]

Turkey was the first Muslim country I had ever been to, and with the dramatic backdrop of the Istanbul mosques lit up at night, the call to prayer was very atmospheric. I happily entered into a city diet of beers and kebabs, not that the opportunity wasn't there to try some other local delicacies. I sampled Turkish coffee in a bar where everyone else seemed much more interested in smoking flavoured water pipes while they played backgammon. This filled the air with a thick aroma, and heading back to the street was a relief as I could breathe more easily. Istanbul felt very much like a compulsory stop for any over-lander heading through the region, a gateway between East and West. As if to prove the point, it wasn't long before we bumped into Nathan, who was the owner of the lone Suzuki. He had also ridden from the UK, and would pop up again on our travels before they were over. He told us his wallet had been stolen as early in his trip as Holland, and that he had also suffered bike problems.

I spent some time looking around the tourist sites of Istanbul. The mosques are very impressive and so is the Grand Bazaar. I preferred the spice bazaar though, it feels more genuine and the back streets around it have an amazing hustle and bustle to them. Every aspect of life is there, happening in the street for all to see. A BBC camera crew were filming a background piece for the Grand Prix in the Grand Bazaar. It's odd to think that they would have flown here in just a few hours against our two week ride. I tried some "real" Turkish delight hoping to find a hidden gem, as I've never been a fan of the odd purple stuff sold in the UK as Turkish delight. However, this stuff wasn't any better as far as I was concerned!

The evenings passed easily in the city's old quarter, near the hostel. In a mainly alcohol free country Sultanamet was an oasis of holiday makers and backpackers taking advantage of the relaxation of restrictions in this area. Getting back to our dormitory at night and finding strangers asleep was odd, and made me long for the privacy and solitude of my little tent. It was strange how protected it made me feel and how much it felt like home after a few weeks of relying on it for shelter.

Before it got too comfortable staying in Istanbul, it was time to move on. We got slightly lost getting on to the right road out as after its finest hour finding the hostel, TomTom wanted to take a ferry. I didn't want to take a ferry however and eventually managed to find the way to the nearest road bridge over the Bosphorus. We ended up on a toll road which was expensive, but a good road for getting some miles under the belt quickly. The only way to pay was to buy a permit for the year. No doubt this is good value if you live locally, but for one-off use felt like a nasty sting. When required we pulled in to fill up with petrol, and were shocked by the expense. It seemed that Turkey was no friend of its oil rich neighbours if the prices were anything to go by. We followed the toll road for a while and then struck out for the coast. On the last straight section of road for miles we collided headlong with one of the many Turkish police speed traps. Both of us were accused, tried and convicted on the spot. Ninety kilometres per hour in a seventy kilometres per hour limit was the crime, although I had seen no signs referring to any speed limit at all. The fine was ninety six lira each. Despite doing my best impression of a friendly and harmless foreigner, all I could get was a photograph with the policeman. No amount of smiling and acting dumb was going to get us away from there without paying up. I wonder if the cash ever made it to the official coffers...

We continued on, and in time the coastline revealed itself as we rounded a bend and the sea stretched out before us giving a brilliant glittering display in the afternoon sun. The skinny coast road was winding and spectacular but slow going. Our plan was to try our hand at wild camping. Inexperienced as we were at that stage, we were too fussy about finding the perfect spot. Before we realised, twilight had turned quickly to darkness. The first place we stopped was surprisingly busy! What looked like an even smaller and little used back road actually had cars coming along regularly. Undeterred we had some dinner at the roadside. Having just eaten a car full of men stopped and began to try and talk to us. It was quickly apparent that we shared no common language, but to me their mannerisms seemed aggressive and very insistent that we should not be there. It was hard to tell if they were angered by our presence or if this was just a cultural difference in the way people communicate. After some tense moments I gathered that they may be trying to warn us. The only logical interpretation I could put to their hand and arm movements was that there was something in the undergrowth that could bite us. At first I thought they meant snakes, but later I remembered that this might be a potential area for ticks to live. I hope this was the case, and that they saved us from being bitten. We packed up hurriedly and carried on in the dark. After what seemed like an age and in an increasingly exhausted state we stopped in a gravelly lay-by. Up ahead we could see the street lights of another town. We had already passed through several just like it. None had thrown up the prospect of anywhere to stay, we were far off the tourist trail by now and hotels and camp grounds were none existent. Rather than end up in conflict with any locals in the town we ended up trying to sleep rough at the side of the road, next to the bikes. The ground was too gravelly and hard to put up the tents. I could hear Al snoring but I couldn't sleep at all. I spent the time reading or writing by the light of my head torch until, in the early hours, the deep red glow of the morning sun began to light the sky.

The first car of the day approached at 4:25am, just as the sun was coming up. The night had been clear, mercifully without rain but a little cold. I reflected on the previous day, in which I had dropped my bike yet again, finding it just too tall and top heavy in slow off road manoeuvres. The rev counter cable came loose too, adding another minor mechanical mishap to the ever growing list. By far the funniest incident from my point of view was that for the first time Al had dropped his bike trying to turn around. Nothing entertaining in itself, I'd done this quite a few times. It was his reaction that made me giggle into my helmet. He was clearly unhurt, but rather than gather himself and simply pick the bike up again he flew into a brief rage. As I looked on from a short distance he tore off his gloves and hurled them theatrically into the ground. It was reminiscent of many motor racing incidents I'd seen where someone is forced out of a race by a competitor or a mechanical failure while winning and is completely distraught about it. I guess I'm lucky that having the odd topple hadn't upset me so much otherwise I'd have been pretty worked up by now with my track record!

After what seemed like miles and miles of passing through the same grim looking Turkish towns the roads gradually improved. I was aiming for Consull Beach, a holiday destination for the Turkish. As we arrived and I pulled over I got an earful from an irate Al who had been following on behind me. I couldn't get any sense out of him in terms of what was wrong at all. What was abundantly clear was that he had decided whatever it was, it was certainly my fault! My best guess was that while I had thought I was having a nice gentle ride along the coast in the sunshine, he felt I was pushing on too far without breaks. In the end I managed to cut through the passive-aggressive hissy fit he was having by suggesting that we turn around and go to see if there was a log cabin available for the night at a place we'd just passed. For a change then, it was early afternoon when we stopped and we got a cabin no problem, which would be a night of relative luxury after last night's shambles. There were fellow over-landers staying, in a monster camper vehicle which looked like it was of military specification, no doubt unstoppable off road! At one hundred Lira it seemed a bit extravagant to me as I would have been happy enough just camping. Nevertheless the bikes were fuelled up for the morning, so there wasn't anything to do but try and enjoy it. To that end I headed down to the beach and lay in the sun. Despite being outside all day every day for weeks I was still pale as I was always covered in the protective bike gear. I managed to buy beer despite it being a Sunday and enjoyed it with some supermarket bought Kofte we cooked on the balcony of the cabin. The evening call to prayer sounded different here, somehow out of place in a beach resort. I spoke to Helen on the phone. She made me feel much better about the row I'd had with Al, which surprised me as of the two of us, she's the more hot-headed one. More than I could have predicted I missed her, and she had become an emotional rock for me to lean on from thousands of miles away.

As always ups followed downs and I had a good time on the road to Erzurum. It is the largest city in and the eponymous capital of Erzurum Province and the city is situated 1757 meters (5766 feet) above sea level. Erzurum had a population of about three hundred and fifty thousand when we were there. Erzurum, known as "The Rock" in NATO code, served as NATO's south-eastern-most air force post during the Cold War. The city uses the double-headed Anatolian Seljuk Eagle as its coat-of-arms, a motif based on the double-headed Byzantine Eagle that was a common symbol throughout Anatolia and the Balkans in the medieval period. It also has some of the finest winter sports facilities in Turkey and hosted the 2011 Winter Universiade.[xi] We didn't see much of that since it was typically hot when we passed through.

It was the little human interactions that were getting really fun this far from home. We stopped at a bank to get more money fairly early one morning and soon gathered an audience. Fascinated by my bike, one kid sat on it for a photograph.

His father motioned me to peer inside a nearby garage. Inside sat a vintage motorbike, evidently his pride and joy. It was a shame not to be able to chat, but the language barrier doesn't get in the way of a mutual love of bikes! Goodwill continued as at the next petrol station the attendants insisted on plying us with free Chai. Drinking tea of various sorts seems to be a popular pastime in more different countries than you might think.

Continuing on good roads, sweeping and well surfaced tarmac, we stopped at a café style place for lunch. There was a reasonably sized outside seating area with a canopy keeping the sun off the diners. It was still quite early, so we had the place pretty much to ourselves. Once again no English was spoken here. However a lunch of Kofte, chai, bread and salad was being prepared fresh in front of our eyes. Two elderly women rolled the Kofte mixture into balls using the palms of their hands before flattening them into a small patty. The owner of the establishment took a good number of these patties and threw them on a charcoal grill at the front of the restaurant. He seemed very pleased that we had decided to choose his place to eat, even though it seemed like about the only option! The food was delicious and plentiful. In fact it was incredibly tasty! While eating and relaxing in the shade, our new friend had opened google earth on his computer and, again through signs, encouraged us to show him where we had come from on our bikes. Suitably refreshed we waddled out into the sunshine and motored away from the coast and into mountains. There were many sections of road works and a crash to keep us on our toes as we rode. After going over a high pass with a war memorial on the top we dropped down and began to look for a place to camp. There had been lots of friendly beeps and waves in this part of Turkey, but there was hassle again when it came time to wild camp. The first place we tried looked like a deserted farm building, but as soon as we arrived another vehicle arrived and warned us off in no uncertain terms. We had better luck at the second attempt. Up a stony track better suited to mountain bikes and not visible from the road, we picked a flatter spot and put up the tents in the failing light. Once dark it felt like nobody would bother us. Although almost unbelievably, one car did come past! This was our first proper wild camp. I fell asleep listening to the crickets on the heathery hillside.

As it turned out, last night's camping spot was next to an army base so it was lucky we weren't spotted and investigated. There is a lot of military activity in Turkey. We couldn't afford to let that put us off though, as we would be wild camping again the next night. The ride through the Usefalli valley was spectacular, but like most places we saw in Turkey, it had been spoiled by man with ugly buildings or rubbish dumped where it shouldn't be. Not only that but it was also due to be flooded to make a reservoir, so as I rode through it I reflected that this route might not be possible for much longer. We came upon a road which was closed due to the work being carried out there, but fortunately it re-opened in forty five minutes time. This seemed a quite common tactic, and people seem resigned to waiting. Most Turkish towns still seemed dirty and dismal with many blocks of flats and shops which reminded me of communist era footage of Russia! The lack of shopping facilities began to show through to the point that we ended up having soup for breakfast as it was all we had left. It wasn't a great start to a day! However, things had looked up by the evening meal so fortunately our camp dinner consisted of meat, bread, cheese and beer. Food of the Gods.

Georgia was on my mind. I knew that tomorrow we'd face another border and more uncertainty, after just about getting used to Turkey. But it would be good to see something new and leave the Jandarma and Polis behind. The bike was still running well apart from an awkward first and second gear selection. It was using a bit of oil too which could have been connected. After another night wild camping I smelt pretty bad! It was tough to stay clean, but at least we had found a reasonable spot. It was right next to the road but behind some trees. The field we were in and the landscape beyond fell away from us and led the eye to a dip in the distant mountain range, which I could only assume was where the border with Georgia would be. Each passing car had beeped hello as we set up camp, so we weren't all that well camouflaged, but none had stopped to bother us. Once under cover of darkness, I once again felt confident we would remain undisturbed.

Georgia

After the almost obligatory daily drop of the bike, this time early on before even reaching the border, I could see we had been close and the mountains did indeed mark the exit from Turkey and entry to Georgia. The paperwork took a while, but was free from charges or bribes and friendly enough. Our map suggested that from the border we would be following the M8 through Georgia. M designates motorway right? Well not here it didn't. The road was more like country B-road in Britain, although we did get to a dual carriageway eventually as we made easy progress towards Tbilisi. Tbilisi, formerly known as Tiflis, is the capital and the largest city of Georgia, lying on the banks of the Mtkvari River with a population of roughly one and a half million inhabitants. Founded in the 5th century by the monarch of Georgia's ancient precursor Kingdom of Iberia, Tbilisi has since served, with intermissions, as the Georgian capital. Formerly, the city had also served as the seat of the Imperial administration of the Caucasus during the Russian rule from 1801 to 1917, the capital of the short-lived Transcaucasian Democratic Federative Republic in 1918, of the Democratic Republic of Georgia from 1918 to 1921, of the Georgian Soviet Socialist Republic from 1921 to 1991, and the Transcaucasian Socialist Federative Soviet Republic from 1922 to 1936.

Located on the south-eastern edge of Europe, Tbilisi's proximity to lucrative east-west trade routes often made the city a point of contention between various rival empires throughout history and the city's location to this day ensures its position as an important transit route for global energy and trade projects. Tbilisi's varied history is reflected in its architecture, which is a mix of medieval, classical, and Soviet structures. Historically, Tbilisi has been home to people of diverse cultural, ethnic, and religious backgrounds, though it is overwhelmingly Eastern Orthodox Christian. Notable tourist destinations include cathedrals like Sameba and Sioni, classical Freedom Square and

Rustaveli Avenue, medieval Narikala Fortress, pseudo-Moorish Opera Theatre, and the Georgian National Museum.[xii]

We failed to see much of the tourist sights. On arrival we tried following signs to the Airport area as we reasoned there was bound to be a selection of hotels. There wasn't a single hotel to be seen anywhere. We were happy to pay for a little luxury after our recent nights roughing it. Asking around near the airport resulted in one shady looking guy volunteering his services. He promised to take us to a good hotel. I was prepared to take a look given the alternatives but Al didn't like the look of him so we lost him in traffic. The drivers here seemed very aggressive and almost hostile towards bikers. Twice cars seemed to swerve towards me as if deliberately trying to scare me or force me into a mistake. Along with the grey buildings and grey skies Georgia left an unfavourable impression on me. It began to rain heavily and with it my bike started playing up. We got stuck travelling along a particular road which took us right past Tbilisi and on to the next town. On asking around we found that the only "hotel" was very, very shut. Heading back to Tbilisi we stopped at the only hotel sign we had seen, even though it has looked very unpromising. It was quite the opposite. They had a reasonably priced twin room, good food, and a bar. The receptionist, who doubled up as the bar maid was very nice and spoke good English. Ups follow downs follow ups.

Azerbaijan

The border crossing from Georgia to Azerbaijan was the longest yet. There were a lot of young soldiers with machine guns. Although they looked pretty menacing it only cost twenty US dollars to get through, so not much corruption in evidence. The road from the border was very bad; an evil mixture of gravel and ruts that meant an accident never seemed far away. A new road was under construction but in the meantime all the heavy construction vehicles were just making the situation worse. Before stopping for our first night in Azerbaijan we had already passed three random police road blocks. Each one raised my heart rate as I wondered if they would find a 'problem' with our documents or accuse us of some other misdemeanours; however all was well. We found a decent hotel in Ganja, otherwise known as Gence, and locked the bikes up around the back out of sight. Gence is Azerbaijan's second-largest city with a population of around three hundred thousand. It was named Elisabethpol in the Russian Empire period. The city regained its original name—Ganja— in 1920 during the first part of its incorporation into the Soviet Union. However, its name was changed again in 1935 to Kirovabad and retained it throughout the later Soviet period from 1935. Finally in 1989, during Perestroika, the city regained the original name.[xiii] The courtyard garden of the hotel even looked as though it might play host to the occasional wedding as the flowers were well kept and the furniture maintained. Most of the rooms were large and arranged off a wide and well lit corridor.

Continuing on our way towards Baku we encountered crazy drivers all the way right along the route. Rules of the road seemed not to matter and even the local dogs joined in chasing us enthusiastically, barking manically all the while. We took a wrong turn somewhere and ended up way to the south of our intended route. This meant we had strayed into a supposed no-go zone. Here we had been told there was risk of being robbed by bandits. It was hard to work out how it could have happened that we had strayed off course as it had seemed as though we had stayed on the main road. Although it was the most major route we could find from West to East across Azerbaijan, there was still a lot of gravel. With tarmac in short supply the bike did well to cope but it didn't stop me worrying about it breaking due to the rough terrain.

Arriving in Baku was a shock. The rest of Azerbaijan was poor. There was no doubt about that, the people looked as though times were hard and the road quality indicated that there was nothing here that mattered. I'd almost crashed about four times myself that day on an extra-muddy section. Baku on the other hand is crazy. Modern hotels, motorways and airport, lots of traffic, expensive cars and shops, even a banner proclaiming the imminent arrival of an Emporio Armani store. Not that any of that helped us. Trying the tactic of heading to the airport to find a hotel failed again. No shortage of accommodation this time, but thanks the oil wealth in Baku even the Holiday Inn was way out of our price range. We ended up in a dump of a hotel, promising ourselves that we would find a better one the following day. The room was large and almost completely bare of any comfort at all, to the extent that it felt like an oversized jail cell.

Baku is the capital and largest city of Azerbaijan, as well as the largest city on the Caspian Sea and of the Caucasus region. Baku is located twenty eight metres or ninety two feet below sea level, which makes it the lowest lying national capital in the world. Baku is also the largest city in the world located below sea level. It is located on the southern shore of the Absheron Peninsula, which projects into the Caspian Sea. The city consists of two principal parts: the down town area and the old Inner City. At the beginning of 2009 shortly before we arrived, Baku's urban population was estimated at just over two million people. Officially, about twenty five percent of all inhabitants of the country live in Baku's metropolitan area. Baku is divided into eleven administrative districts or "raions" and 48 townships. Among these are the townships on islands in the Baku Bay and the town of Oil Rocks built on stilts in the Caspian Sea, sixty kilometres away from Baku. The Inner City of Baku along with the Shirvanshah's Palace and Maiden Tower were inscribed as a UNESCO

World Heritage Site in 2000. According to the Lonely Planet's ranking, Baku is also among the world's top ten destinations for urban nightlife.

The city is the scientific, cultural and industrial centre of Azerbaijan. Many sizeable Azerbaijani institutions have their headquarters there, including SOCAR, one of the world's top 100 companies and others. The rather grandly named Baku International Sea Trade Port, sheltered by the islands of the Baku Archipelago to the east and the Absheron Peninsula to the north, is capable of handling two million tons of general and dry bulk cargoes per year.[xiv] Finding a better hotel in Baku wasn't a prospect that filled me with joy. Not only that, but we also needed to find our way to the port. Our only way out of Baku, other than the way we had come, was to get a boat across the Caspian Sea. More than any other, this was the part of the route where it could all go wrong. The immediate need was to get our bikes placed into customs at the port because the bikes, unlike us, only had three day transit visas. Lord only knows why they have to make it so short! Such lofty concerns as not falling foul of immigration rules and causing an international incident rubbed alongside day to day problems like the inevitable athletes foot which had set in. I was trying to treat it but the cream I was using had its work cut out in the hot damp environment of my bike boots! In retrospect, the ferry was always the bit of the trip I feared the most. If I had been more single minded during the planning stage perhaps we would have ignored the expense, and gone ahead to buy a carnet allowing us passage through Iran. I wasn't sure how that would have worked out with getting a 'tour' in Turkmenistan though. A guided tour was the only way to officially pass through Turkmenistan, making it pretty expensive. Either way it was pretty academic by that point. I had lots of mixed feelings at the time, not something I wanted when trying to enjoy the Big Trip (™). I just had to trust that I would feel better when we got into Turkmenistan and successfully met up with our guides. I managed to find a cash machine which worked and went into a bar with my new found wealth. The beers were about five pounds a pint, more expensive than the UK! This really was a weird and exclusive outpost in the middle of nowhere. It certainly felt a long way from home as the odometer clicked around to five thousand two hundred miles covered.

Belying all of the trepidation I felt about finding a suitable hotel and the right part of the port, serendipity swung into action and produced one of those amazing travel days that you read about but can't quite believe would ever happen to you. It started with me coming up with the idea to return to a hotel we had stopped at on the way into Baku. This was a very classy looking establishment and had been far too expensive to stay at. I'm not sure why, but I felt that they were much more likely to help than anyone else in our current position. The receptionist couldn't reduce the price enough for us to stay, but he said that another member of staff, who had just finished their shift and left to go home was a keen biker and would love to help two foreign bikers in need. His name was Farid. To his eternal credit, on getting the call Farid turned around and came back to meet us. He was instantly friendly and took the initiative. Yes this place was too expensive, but he also worked at another hotel in the centre of town. Of all things, it was called the Red Lion. He would take us there and negotiate a special rate. Normally this might ring a few alarm bells to the cynical European, but this really seemed to be a case of the international community of bikers coming to the rescue. Farid set off at pace on his Yamaha Fazer with us struggling to keep up but in hot pursuit, determined not to get left behind in the heavy traffic. When we got there the hotel was great, we had a suite style room and there was a pub style bar downstairs. Farid then took us to the port and helped us by translating with customs and buying tickets. I found it totally amazing and heart-warming that a total stranger took so much time, with no advance notice at all, just to help. Finally our saviour arranged to take us out to his favourite kebab place for dinner. While we were at the port customs post, Nathan whom we had met back in Istanbul rolled up. It seemed like a small world after all, particularly when shortly after another Brit called Russ arrived on his BMW 800. We were all looking for a boat out of Baku.

Leaving the port we spent the rest of the day getting our bearings and seeing the sights of Baku. Later in the evening we had what passed for big night out, going to several bars with Nathan and Russ. After all, this was supposed to be one of the top ten world destinations for urban night life, so it would have been rude not to. It was nice to have different company and take things a bit less seriously for a while. The next day was due to be a national holiday, so it wouldn't be possible to do much as most places would be closed. Not that there was much left to do but wait. It was Sunday and we hoped that the boat was going to depart on Tuesday. I spoke to Helen on the phone, but it was difficult because she asked if I would try and text her more and I'd made the mistake of telling her I kept forgetting. She didn't take this well. The fact was that in her mind we were just chilling in Baku and this made her feel like she was being forgotten about all the way back home. She was upset and there didn't seem to be anything I could do to make her feel better. The rest of the time in Baku passed slowly. Farid hadn't shown up for dinner as we'd arranged, but in another moment of chance we saw him in the street and found out why. His brother had borrowed his motorbike and crashed it, so this emergency had obviously come first. It turned out that the motorbike was badly damaged but his brother was OK, so we rearranged for dinner the next evening. Before that came around however, our good fortune took a turn for the worse. I got very ill. Something I had eaten resulted in a nasty bout of nausea and diarrhoea. I struggled out to meet Farid for dinner, keen to say thank you for all his help and enjoy some local knowledge of the best place in town. I stayed off the beer and got some fresh air, but I was feeling so sick that I couldn't enjoy dinner with Farid and his friends. He prescribed very sharp tasting local yoghurt as the best thing to fix my ailing stomach and I ate as much as I dared. I don't know if it helped and I just prayed silently for a quick recovery. The morning of departure came and I had to focus on getting to the ferry and on with the journey.

The Caspian Sea

I hadn't seen the young chap at hotel reception before and as we tried to check out of the Red Lion he tried to charge us nearly $800! This was way more than we had agreed. He also suggested we could pay in the local currency, 717 Manat. A quick calculation revealed that the two prices were nowhere near an equal amount, but we had no chance to pay in the local currency as we didn't have enough left. Eventually after another call to Farid, an explanation of the original deal to the receptionist got the rate back down to less than half the amount he had tried to charge us and to roughly the agreed price. We arrived at the port bright and early on the 16th June, keen that there was no chance the ferry would take off without us and leave us stranded for another week. We had never been given any indication of what time the ferry would go. In fact, the term ferry could only be very loosely applied. In reality this was a cargo ship, which didn't usually take any passengers. On enquiring, the man who had sold us our tickets a few days earlier indicated that even though it had arrived, it was too windy for the boat to dock, and to come back in two hours. Without anywhere particular to go, we waited with the bikes, trying to screen my eyes from the dust picked up by the gusty breeze, until about 11:30am. Since it was well over his suggested two hours, we tried again. He obviously felt that another round of mimes wasn't going to get the message across sufficiently, so he called his English speaking daughter on the phone to explain to me that now the ferry wouldn't go until 5pm. Disappointed and frustrated we headed to the 'Golden Pub' to kill time, and ordered two coffees on entry. We failed to be able to order anything else in the next two hours. This had to be the 'World's Worst Waitress' grand prize winner. So resolute was her determination to ignore us that we left hungry and annoyed. A search for a better café or eatery failed and we ended up with a lunch of crisps and chocolate. This was followed some hours later by bread and processed cheese triangles for dinner. Not one of the great culinary adventures the world has to offer! The wind gradually got worse and worse. At some random point during the afternoon one member of the Polis calls my name out. He photocopies our passports and gives us back our V5 bike registration documents. Another check with the ticket man, more in hope than expectation, and he now says 7-8pm. We can see ships, one of which is meant to be the ferry, although they all look like the same model. Around 7pm, probably because he is going off duty, the ticket man decides he will issue our tickets. He makes a big show of reducing the $210 dollar "price" to $190 each, which Farid had already told us he had negotiated days ago. He wrote the tickets, and then bizarrely gave me $10 back "for vodka". This little act of kindness I think means he likes us; that and the fact that a flashing smile revealed his gold teeth!

Eventually, with darkness approaching, the ferry charges up towards the landing bay and docks with the aid of a tug. The wind is the same as ever. There's no way that it's any less windy that it had been first thing this morning! Nothing happened for a long time, but then some foot passengers get off. We wait. Three lorries crawl off and are very slowly searched by the world's worst trained sniffer dog. He seemed more interested in doing just about anything rather than looking for drugs! We wait. Two noisy diesel train engines shunt couplings right up to the boat and hitch up the cargo and pull it off. The tracks are built right into the boat and link up with those on the dock. Then they replace that cargo with some to be taken back the other way. After what seemed like an age, the port "patron" announces himself to us. He demands $10 from each of us and is going nowhere and doing nothing without it, so we pay up. Upon forking out he signals to kick off passport control. They motion that we are to put our luggage through their fancy metal detector/scanner. This is obviously their pride and joy. We take just enough off the bikes to look like it could be everything, if you didn't bother looking outside at the bikes! In reality the whole exercise was totally pointless as both bikes still had their panniers in place. After all, mine would take a considerable time with a spanner to remove. We then proceed to a huge misunderstanding when they keep on asking Al for another ticket. It looks like the ticket only mentions the bike? It turns out they just want to see my ticket! I don't know why sign language doesn't seem to work here! After that everyone is all smiles again, other than one official thinking that Al's GPS device was a radio and wanting the declaration. Radio's must be declared in this part of the world, but after we try everything we can think of in English to explain that it isn't necessary, he seems to give up. There's just one more office to go. One guard enters passport details into the computer and asks for a $20 'present' for his boss. We act dumb and get away with it. Sometimes it's hard to know what is a bribe and what is a legitimate fee, but this one is pretty obvious and that makes it much easier to stall until they get bored trying. We finally ride bikes onto ferry and use our tie downs to secure them in the cargo hold with a mix of excitement at being aboard and concern as to whether we will stay floating long enough to make it to the other side. The captain checks our tickets and it seems we've already paid $20 for a cabin. He then disappears with our passports. The cabin is disgusting and the toilets are worse. The cabin doesn't include such luxuries as a blanket or pillow, but we end up getting them for free by claiming lack of money. It's not like we really wanted to use them anyway. The toilet reminded me of the suppository scene in Trainspotting (had that scene also come with smell-o-vison) where Ewan McGregor goes into what is labelled the worse toilet in Scotland. Well, that may have been the case, but I think what stood in front of me would easily win the award for the worst toilet in the world. The worst I have ever seen, before or since. That includes many that were simply holes in the ground. At least they were usually well ventilated. This was like being in a hot rusty tin can swimming in urine and smeared with faeces. The smell was overpowering and it was all I could do not to vomit. This isn't the ideal situation when you've got an upset stomach.

Traumatized by the toilet later in the voyage I resorted to peeing in an empty coke bottle. By that time I would be pretty dehydrated, and my orange pee might still be floating around the Caspian for all I know. The ship had finally sailed at 17/6/09 at 03:00 on 17/6/09. Just eighteen hours wait to catch a ferry! The whole ferry crossing was supposed to take fifteen hours. My diary from the time on the ferry shows an increasing sense of desperation and extreme boredom!

17/6/09 - 10:30, no land in sight.

Forgot to mention, I lost my tax disk somewhere, loose bolt.

17/6/09 - 13:05 – No land in sight.

From Eastern Europe on, I've encountered the following on the roads – dead dogs and cats, live cows, sheep, dogs, horses, donkeys, goats, "Stelvio Gophers" and pigs.

18/6/09 – 09:30

I spotted land and then we anchored with other waiting ships last night about 6pm. We haven't moved since. So that's... 30.5 hours on the ferry so far. For a 15 hour crossing! We travel at about 12.5 mph when we're going, measured with my GPS. I slept for 8-9 hours

18/6/09 12:10 – No movement

18/6/09 18:10 – No movement – 24 hours on the spot

Apparently there is another ship in the dock, so we can't go in. We will dock, and I quote "Maybe this evening". I got a crew member to take me down into the hold to the bikes. I retrieved another meal, some sweets and water. This is getting quite bad as we were running out of food and water, there were no facilities to buy anything on board and no help was forthcoming from the crew. They spent their time lazily fishing off the side of the ship. I didn't spend much time on deck. It smelt better and fresher but it seemed to be shrouded in a cloud of huge flies which wouldn't leave me alone.

Not surprisingly, a mobile signal in the bowels of a cargo ship was non-existent and I was aware that the SPOT tracker would have been showing us in the same place for days on end. As far as anyone watching that would be concerned I could well have been lying at the bottom of the Caspian Sea. Amazingly I'd popped up on deck for some much needed fresh air and no sooner had I switched my phone on when it started to ring. My need for fresh air had coincided with Helen's wake up time for work, and having seen still no contact from me, she tried calling on the off chance. It was good to speak to her so she could pass on reassurances to the rest of the family, but my exasperation at the whole situation on the boat, mixed with dehydration and tiredness made me snap at her. Sadly, in my mind, I had bigger problems to worry about than how she was coping.

18/6/09 - 19:50 – We're moving! And have been for a while. We will hopefully dock in the next 30 minutes!!!

Turkmenistan

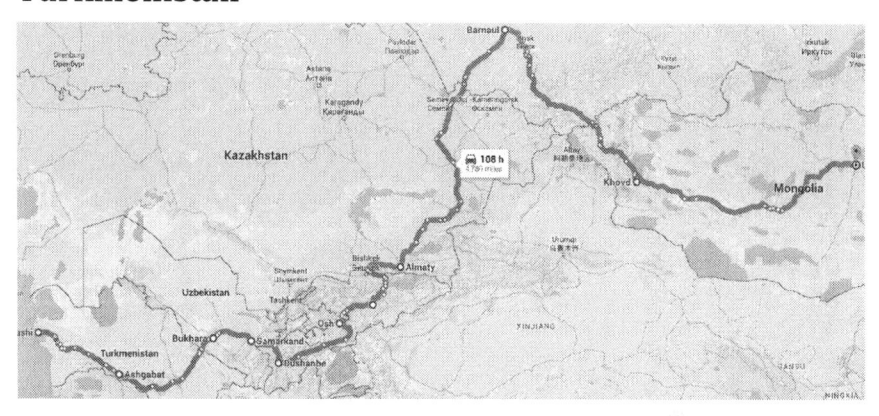

Ferry finally docked in Turkmenbashi port by about 9pm, a mammoth forty two hour crossing. It wasn't over then however; the border formalities were long and convoluted and took until about 00:45 on the 19th, basically three days after setting out. They were expensive too, even refusing the obvious attempts to get a bribe all of the paperwork cost $110, and this was on top of the visa we had already bought back in the UK which was nestled in our passports. During this process we met up with our tour guide Mucsat and our driver who, true to their word, had come to find us when the ship came in. I finally got to bed about 1:45am in the half decent "Hotel Turkmenbasy". It was a pretty grand high rise sort of place. But appearances aren't everything and there was only running water at certain times of the day. I.e. not this time of day!

Turkmenbashi has had a difficult history. In 1717, Russian Prince Alexander Bekovich-Cherkassky landed and established a secret fortified settlement on this location, where the dry bed of a former mouth of the Amu-Darya River once emptied into the Caspian Sea. His intent was to march an army up this dry riverbed and conquer the Khanate of Khiva. The expedition failed, and the Russians abandoned the settlement for over 150 years. In 1869, the Russians invaded a second time. They named their fort Krasnovodsk, which is the Russian version of the original name, Kyzyl-Su (Red Water). Krasnovodsk was Imperial Russia's base of operations against Khiva and Bukhara, and the nomadic Turkmen tribes.

In 1993, Krasnovodsk was renamed by President for Life Saparmurat Niyazov, after his self-proclaimed title Türkmenbaşy ("Leader of all Turkmen"). Niyazov's successor Gurbanguly Berdimuhamedow pledged, in July 2007, to invest one billion dollars into a project slated to turn Türkmenbaşy into a major tourist resort – the centre of the Avaza Tourist Zone with 60 modern hotels to be built along a sixteen kilometre stretch of the Caspian Sea shoreline.[xv] I'm not quite sure I saw a billion dollars' worth of development just yet.

I had a forgettable omelette again for breakfast before setting off on what became an unforgettable day. After leaving Turkmenbashi we rode through real desert all day. This was true dunes and sandstorms country and a stunning place to be.

Our guides were using a 4X4 and we followed on the bikes. The heat was incredible, 40 degrees plus was showing on my thermometer. Over the couple of hundred miles we covered my laundry that I'd diligently hand washed at the hotel and tied on my bike to dry in the wind, fell off, never to be seen again. That day the desert claimed one T-Shirt, one pair of socks and one pair of Calvin Klein boxer shorts; my only hope is that there's a well-dressed camel roaming around there! Speaking of which, there were many trains of camels wandering around freely, making the scene exotic and almost biblical. As the sun began to set we turned a corner and I couldn't believe my eyes. In the valley below, spread out like a shimmering white city from some alien planet, was Ashgabat. Ashgabat is the capital of, and the largest city in Turkmenistan, situated between the Kara Kum desert and the Kopet Dag mountain range. The 2009 census estimated a population of 1 million, primarily Turkmen people, with ethnic minorities of Russians, Armenians and Azerbaijanis. It is 250 kilometres from the second largest city in Iran, Mashhad.

The Karakum Canal runs through the city, carrying waters from the Amu Darya from east to west. Each building seemed to have its orderly place and each looked as though it was made of pure white granite. They seemed to like building things here to show the rest of the world that they were important. For example, the Alem Cultural and Entertainment Centre was recognised by Guinness World Records as the world's tallest Ferris wheel in an enclosed space. The Ashgabat Flagpole is the fourth tallest free-standing flagpole in the world, standing at one hundred and thirty three metres tall. The Ashgabat Fountain is made up of the world's greatest number of fountain pools in a public place. Ashgabat also features Turkmenistan Tower which is the tallest tower in Turkmenistan, and the decorative octagonal Star of Oguzkhan which is recognized as the world's largest architectural image of the star and entered in the Guinness World Records.[xvi]

Like Baku, after riding through miles of nothingness the capital came as a shock. Turkmenistan was being run by a dictatorial leader and clearly this was where he had chosen to spend the money. I was riding towards this extraordinary sight at the back of our little convoy, with the sleeves of my bike jacket flapping in the breeze in an attempt to keep me cool. Now that the sun had lost its strength for the day it was starting to work and I was enjoying the cold draft reaching up my arms. Suddenly there was a sharp pain in my right forearm. I swerved violently off to the side of the road and brought the bike to a stop as hard as I could. I leapt off and tore off my jacket. A quick look at my arm revealed a puncture wound, but gingerly exploring the arm of my jacket didn't reveal the insect that had made it. It felt like an extremely painful wasp sting, and my arm began to swell and turn red. The rest of the group had noticed my absence and swung around to look for me. I rejoined them and shortly after made it to the Hotel Acia. This place was recognisable as a western style hotel too with restaurant prices to match. Unfortunately the quality of my steak did not match the expense. I eased the pain in my arm with a few bottles of cold Russian beer. All of Turkmenistan seemed like a desert and I couldn't help wonder why before the days of finding oil or gas, anyone would choose to make their home in such a harsh environment. The ride through the desert had taken its toll on the bikes too. Al had lost the chain guard from his bike and in odd symmetry mine was also ripped to pieces. The only other bikers we had seen were wearing huge white hoods, presumably to protect them from the sun. It made them look like members of an American white supremacy group. Overall it was just a great feeling to be off the ferry, away from the shocking conditions and no longer trapped!

The next stop on our "guided tour" was a crater in the desert which is permanently on fire, fuelled by natural gas leaking to the surface. The crater we were told had been formed by an accident with weak ground and heavy equipment during gas exploration. The gas has ignited and has resisted any attempts to put it out. This was an exciting prospect but all was not well. Waking in the morning the realisation dawned that my diarrhoea was back. It seemed like this had been going on forever and I was beginning to wonder if my digestion would ever be normal again. To add injury to insult, more insect bites on my neck were emerging to complement my badly swollen arm. There was now a big sore and red blotch there. The day further developed into what may have been the most uncomfortable of my life! Once again there was full on sand dune desert, mega heat, an inability to hydrate due to the temperature and bad stomach combination. Then the last straw came when our guides wanted us to ride seven kilometres over very soft sand to the crater. Al and I both got stuck a few times in the first few yards and quickly implemented 'plan B'. We left the bikes at a checkpoint and jumped in the 4X4. The sole purpose of the manned checkpoint seemed to be to stop any accidents where the road crossed a railway. This turned out to be the best decision ever, as we were both physically spent.

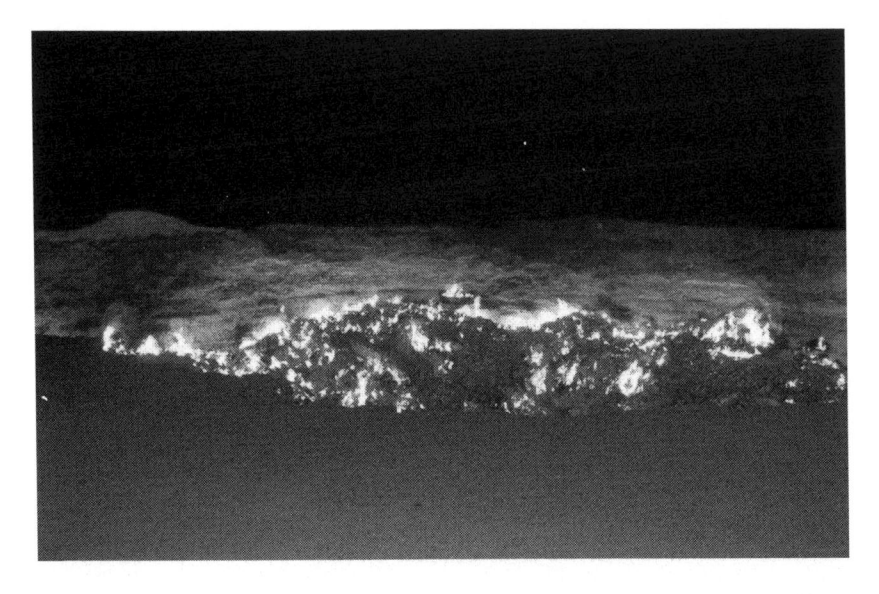

The gas crater is very impressive and looks good at night. You can smell the gas and feel the heat! I was feeling too rough to have much of the camp dinner of chicken, salad and roast tomatoes. Or even any of the free vodka! Al got suddenly ill with similar symptoms to those I had already been experiencing, and spent the night with diarrhoea and vomiting. A couple who were both Slovakian medical graduates had arrived with another set of tour guides and we chatted over dinner. The Slovakian's wanted to talk politics and pushed the guides over their attitudes towards their country's leader. Even though the guides were all friends they would not be drawn into saying anything negative about the political situation. I got the impression that they were far from positive about their non-democratic system, but were too scared to say anything in case we were spies or journalists. We all sat on several rugs laid out on the sand. Above us a single electric light, powered from the car, cast a dim light and created deep shadows. I was just thinking that I couldn't really see what I was trying to eat when something landed on my back with a thump. The light had attracted many insects and out here in the desert they were massive. I shook off, what I could only assume in the darkness was some kind of grasshopper, cricket or locust. It felt like the size and weight of a small garden bird. After that I was glad to get into my tent and be protected from the creatures of the night by the mesh of the inner tent. On this night the weather was so warm and the chance of rain so remote I didn't put up the outer waterproof layer of the tent to try and get a little cooling breeze through the tent. The guides slept on the ground in the open, seemingly impervious to all varieties of creepy crawly.

The next morning it became clear that Al was too weak to ride his bike. With my help we eventually got him and his gear packed up and into the 4X4. Back at the bikes I paid the guard four Manat for looking after the bikes. There was another local at the checkpoint when we were looking to solve the problem of getting Al and his bike to the border before our visas ran out and we illegally overstayed our welcome. Via our guide the stranger offered to ride it to the border for two hundred Manat. The small gathering of Turkmen must have really wondered what strange bargaining tactic I was about to employ, as without warning, I yelped and hurriedly pulled down my biking trousers! I had felt a sharp sting at the back of my left knee. In the folds of my trousers I saw something wriggling and writhing and flicked at it with my fingers. Much to my relief whatever it was popped out and onto the ground. My relief was short lived as I saw what had caused the sting. It was a scorpion. It must have crawled up my trouser leg as I was standing there. It was a silvery white colour and almost translucent. I hadn't felt it move at all. As soon as it hit the ground one of the locals stamped on it. I had no idea how dangerous this sting might be. I knew some scorpion bites could be fatal, but there was no panic on the faces of those around me. One of the guys went around the back of the checkpoint building, which was like a small concrete shed not dissimilar to a bus shelter. He came back and presented me with a scrap of material soaked in petrol, and motioned to wipe it on the wound. I wasn't sure how this was going to help, but I followed his instructions and the pain began to ease. In the end the sting caused no further problems and was nowhere near as bad as the sting on my arm that I'd already picked up.

Drama over, Mucsat bargained the price of the mystery rider's time up to 240 Manat, about eighty five US dollars, for reasons totally beyond my comprehension. Now it seemed that this guy would happily do his fellow countryman a favour at the expense of his paying clients. I wasn't happy but without any other options we did the deal and rode to Urguch, near the border. On the way I had to pull over twice when I could last no longer. Each time I would run off behind the nearest sand dune, crouch down and let forth a torrent of liquid very comparable to silage at high pressure from my back side. The large local dung beetles would then appear from nowhere and clear away the stinking slick from the sand with startling speed and efficiency. All this happened despite the fact that I had eaten nothing more than a single biscuit all day. The only relief from the heat and discomfort came when a simple building emerged from the heat haze like a modern day oasis. It was a café of sorts, with an ancient refrigerator cooling two litre bottles of fizzy drinks. I selected a violent green coloured drink with pictures of apples on the front and tipped the ice cold liquid down my throat. The super-strong artificial apple favour combined with the cold was such a joy I've never forgotten it.

Nearing, but not at the border, although he was still feeling weak, Al had to get back on his bike because our new found friend refused to go any further. It looked as though we were entering a more built up area and either this guy had a traffic light phobia, or he was worried about being spotted by someone? Having spent every last Manat, we managed to exit Turkmenistan. This was pretty tedious for an exit from a country. The exit is almost always much faster and easier than an entry so the border guards know you will be someone else's problem shortly. We entered Uzbekistan enduring their very thorough customs procedures in the heat of the day, but without getting ripped off any further. The first decent sized town from the border is Nukus. Nukus is the sixth-largest city in Uzbekistan, and the capital of the autonomous Karakalpakstan Republic. The Amu Darya river passes west of the town. The city is best known for its world-class Nukus Museum of Art, but you wouldn't know from the look or feel of the town, it feels pretty basic. The name Nukus is associated with the old tribal name Uzbeks - Nukus. Nukus developed from a small settlement in 1932 into a large, modern Soviet city with broad avenues and big public buildings by the 1950s. The city's isolation made it host to the Red Army's Chemical Research Institute, a major research and testing centre for chemical weapons. With the fall of the Soviet Union and the growing environmental disaster of the Aral Sea, the city's situation has deteriorated. Contamination of the region by wind-borne salt and pesticides from the dry Aral Sea bed have turned the surrounding area into a wasteland, with very high rates of respiratory disorders, cancer, birth defects and deformities.[xvii] We stumbled our way to the 'Nukus Hotel'. I was very drained arriving in Uzbekistan. We changed plans to stay an additional night here in order for Al to recover. I had two other things on my mind: Firstly the need to work on the bike because the electrics were playing up and secondly considering whether I could eat without initiating instant diarrhoea.

Uzbekistan

Our first day in Nukus was spent recovering from the ordeal that Turkmenistan had turned out to be. Having to cover so many miles, in extreme heat, with poor health and under tight time pressure had been very challenging. As usual, there was something else to pile on a bit more discomfort. Overnight I had gained at least thirty insect bites, so after the horse had bolted I set up my mosquito net for the following night. Although large, this was by far the worst hotel of the entire trip. Our room was stiflingly hot and humid, and it stank like sewage. Our collective bowel movements did nothing to improve that situation. A lot of time was spent with Al just resting while I watched the only channel which was vaguely understandable. It was a dreadful English/Italian music channel. I looked on in increasing boredom since the same songs from Dizzee Rascal, Lady Gaga, Eminem and Kelly Rowland were on heavy rotation! It was particularly odd to hear Dizzee Rascal's London accent on television so far some home.

To get out of the hotel we went back to a bazaar I had found on a brief exploration the previous evening. We changed some money, 65 Euros is 135,000 "sum". We got it all in one thousand notes, meaning that I ended up with a huge wedge of notes. I tried to buy some 'safe' food and had a breakfast of fried egg, hot dog sausage and bread in the hotel which was OK. I felt better by this stage apart from still having very loose bowel movements. Al was still suffering. I was praying that he would make a speedy recovery, so that we could try and set off the next day and escape the delightful dump, Hotel Nukus! Unfortunately there was no such luck; Al had a bad night so we were forced to stay another day. Thankfully things looked up a little as we managed to change rooms to one with air conditioning and which didn't smell of poo. I couldn't believe that they hadn't let us have this room to start with as the hotel seemed to have few or maybe no other guests but we had never been given the option. Lastly, in one final quirk, the hotel mysteriously ran out of sugar for my morning chai. Some justice was done when we managed to skip paying the 12000sum bike parking charge.

When we set off from Nukus, our intention was to camp halfway to Bukhara, the next town on our route. The terrain put an end to that idea. It was all desert, very hot and very inhospitable, with no shelter at all! The best we could do was stop under a rail bridge in the heat of the day. Our only reasonable option seemed to be to push on to Bukhara, about 350 miles away in total. Al struggled all the way. We were an attraction wherever we stopped. Curious locals would pop out of the woodwork to take a look at the crazy foreigners. There were lots of police checkpoints, and we were stopped at some of them, but they never carried out a document check or anything else.

Uzbekistan seems to have more animals above insect size than Turkmenistan, maybe being a little further North there was a little more water and a slightly kinder climate. The engine noise of the bikes would upset trains of camels which ran off into the desert. Little lizards and geckos darted onto the road from the verge. There were the ever present dogs too, one of which was hit by a car coming the other way when it ran out to chase us! I was glad to be on the road again after Nukus, but even more glad to reach Bukhara. Bukhara is the capital of the Bukhara Province of Uzbekistan and is more like museum than a city, with about a hundred and forty monuments of architecture. The nation's fifth-largest city, it has a population of over a quarter of a million people. The region around Bukhara has been inhabited for at least five millennia, and the city has existed for half that time. Located on the Silk Road, the city has long been a centre of trade, scholarship, culture, and religion. The historic centre of Bukhara, which contains numerous mosques and madrassas, has been listed by UNESCO as a World Heritage Site.[xviii] After a once around the new town we found the older hotel section. At random we chose the Amelia boutique hotel which was lovely. It had an old Silk Road style, but with modern convenience and standards including wireless internet! Breakfast was fruit, yoghurt, rice pudding, plum jam, sesame biscuits, tea, coffee, potato donuts and pancakes! The best so far and in total contrast to Nukus! They even let us wheel the motorbikes down the narrow passageway and into the courtyard of the hotel just below our room for security.

While in our hotel room in Bukara, I switched on the TV which had the BBC world service as one of the channels. The news came through that Michael Jackson was dead. It was the top story on BBC world and had wall to wall coverage. My mind wandered home, as I knew Helen and her friend Janine had tickets to see him in London. She'd been super excited about the show, having been a massive fan for years and never having seen him live; now that it wouldn't be happening, I wondered how she would be feeling. I got bored of the wall to wall coverage of what were essentially the same facts surrounding his death and went out for a walk on my own. In the centre of town I got chatting to a guy who wanted to take me to show his two hundred year old house where his wife would cook dinner. It didn't seem unsafe, so trying to be open to all the new experiences I could, I went along. When I arrived there I got the hard sell on some mini carpets! The price went from $30 to $20 as I reiterated that I was travelling by motorbike and carrying a carpet didn't seem like the most practical idea. So there was no sale for him on this occasion. His house seemed to be mainly one room with just carpets on the floor. I soaked up the marketplace and ancient passageways of Bukara and walked around the castle. Once I got on the internet I caught up with some practicalities, like checking my bank accounts in case my details and been taken anywhere and used for fraud, or more likely I'd spent more than I thought! It was also useful for finding out more up to date information about hotels in Samarkand and the top things to see when we got there. When I spoke to Helen on the phone I found that I really missed her now. Bukara was kind of magical and it would have been wonderful to share that with her.

An inspection of the current state of the bikes revealed that the luggage racks on both had snapped near the exhaust and the odd other random bolt had disappeared. By this stage we were undeterred by such trifles and set off towards Samarkand anyway. It was an easy ride, so we were in a hotel by 3pm. It was quite a nice hotel, but also fairly expensive and their promised internet connection was not working. On the road we had entered the land of the Daewoo. There were an amazing number of Daewoo Matiz and Nexia cars here. This seemed to mark a change in the direction from which goods and influence was flowing. Of course it was hard not to notice the cars as lots of them were being driven the wrong way up the dual carriageway towards me! This certainly focusses the mind. The country between Bukara and Samarkand is largely farmed and quite pleasant. We walked around Samarkand taking in the sights and sounds. Samarkand is the second-largest city in Uzbekistan and the capital of Samarqand Province. The city is most noted for its central position on the Silk Road between China and the West, and for being an Islamic centre for scholarly study. In the 14th century it became the capital of the empire of Timur (Tamerlane) and is the site of his mausoleum (the Gur-e Amir). The Bibi-Khanym Mosque remains one of the city's most notable landmarks although it is a modern replica. The Registan was the ancient centre of the city. The city has carefully preserved the traditions of ancient crafts: embroidery, gold embroidery, silk weaving, engraving on copper, ceramics, carving and painting on wood.

In 2001, UNESCO added the city to its World Heritage List as Samarkand – Crossroads of Cultures.[xix] The Gur e Amir was just down the street from the hotel. Much more impressive though were the "big two", the Registan and the Bibi-Khanym Mosque. The old traditional tiling on these buildings is fantastically intricate and the bold blue porcelain pops brilliantly in the bright sunshine. Near the Bibi-Khanym Mosque there is a huge food market selling all kinds of fresh food. It was a shame that the language difference really was a barrier in these situations. Although pointing works pretty well to establish what you want, as nothing is in a packet or portion, it is tough to indicate whether you want a gram or a tonne. In addition, these places are set up for home dwellers not travellers. We generally wanted a complete meal or snack to eat there and then, whereas mostly raw ingredients were for sale which needed combining and cooking. We had neither the facilities nor the will for this. Where possible I tried to make up for this by trying local dishes in restaurants, and Samarkand was particularly notable for its excellent Shasklik, a type of meat kebab. Before we left Samarkand there was time for some bike maintenance outside the front of the hotel. I fixed all of the indicators where the wiring had shaken loose, replaced a blown headlight bulb and removed the snapped piece of luggage rack to stop it jangling around. Finally I washed and oiled my bikes aftermarket air filters.

Tajikistan

The next target was Lake Iskander and we got up and left with no problems until reaching the border. We were missing a yellow form to exit Uzbekistan. Other than it being yellow, I am still none the wiser about what this form was for or why we didn't have it. It caused quite a fuss but in the end we got out of the country anyway without a search or indeed a penalty of any kind. We also completed the procedure for entry into Tajikistan with no problems and no customs search. In fact the whole process took less than two hours and only cost fifteen dollars. Seemed like great going for a border crossing in this part of the world. Once over the border there were smiles and waves from the locals on all sides, despite the Uzbekistan customs official ominously pronouncing that we would definitely be shot from the hills.

Gun toting bandits were not in evidence, but that didn't mean everything was to go smoothly. I had big bike trouble. It just would not fire properly, like it was wet but it wasn't. It had been a pig all day hence we were a few km short of our target of Lake Iskander. Iskanderkul is a mountain lake of glacial origin in Tajikistan's Sughd Province. It lies at an altitude of 2,195 metres on the northern slopes of the Gissar Range in the Fann Mountains. Triangular in shape, it has a surface area of 3.4 square kilometres and is up to 72 metres deep. Claimed to be one of the most beautiful mountain lakes in the former Soviet Union, it is a popular tourist destination. The lake takes its name from Alexander the Great: Iskander is the Persian pronunciation of Alexander, and kul is lake in Tajik, which is of Turkic origin.

The outflow of the lake is the Iskander Darya, which joins the Yaghnob River to form the Fan Darya, a major left tributary of the Zeravshan River.[xx] Deciding the best thing to do was stop and repair the bike tomorrow, we set up our tents for another wild camp. The route to Lake Iskander was a detour off the main route and the bike finally conked out conveniently close to a fairly large and flat patch of land in a sheltered valley. We would be clearly visible but the road was little used. The idea had been to spend the night at the lake then push on to Dushanbe the following day. That would all depend on getting the bike going. Reverting to type we had a dinner of pasta, tomato and tuna made on the camp stove. There was nothing much to do in the dark but get an early night in readiness for an early start. Running through the valley, just the other side of the gravelly road from the camp was a rushing river, swollen with icy cold melt-water from the surrounding mountains. Some of the mountains further into the distance had snow on them. Being stranded at the side of the road with a broken bike was a pretty sharp contrast to the relatively luxurious hotels we had enjoyed recently. At least we had plenty of cold running water!

The next day was all spent trying to make the bike work. In retrospect it should have been obvious that the problem was related to my ill-conceived attempted at maintenance the previous day. By this stage though, so many mechanical and electrical hitches had come along that it seemed like it could be anything. That said we did establish that this time the electrics weren't at fault and it seemed to be fuel or air related. At one point we thought we had cracked it by removing the air filters. The "clean" I had done didn't seem to have helped and re-oiling them only made them stickier and more clogged by all the dirt and dust that was flying around. The problem came back. By this time we were pulling parts from the running bike and swapping them over to try and isolate the problem, with lots of our investigations involving the carburettor. A lunch of noodles came and went. Time passed trying ever more potential fixes. When the time came, it was more noodles and canned fish plus half a chocolate bar for dinner. We decided that we would have to try to get to Dushanbe tomorrow regardless, even if this meant towing. If that was too hazardous on the rough terrain I thought we may need to flag down a truck and negotiate to put the bike on the back. In the end though we spent the whole day frustrated, trying to get the bike to run.

We really needed the bike to run to be able to make it out of Tajikistan on the right side of the customs deadline. Once again visa deadlines were tight. Technology wasn't helping us either. There was no mobile signal in the valley. The laptop was not working to view the parts catalogue or manual we had stored away on it. In my mind I was running through all kinds of scenarios if the bike couldn't be made to run, from buying an old Lada and continuing my journey in that, to flying home. I knew one thing though; I didn't want to stop the adventure here. I felt I had only just recovered from being ill and I desperately wanted to see Mongolia! At least, I thought with a smile, being here was a thousand times better than being on that ferry, or even in Hotel Nukus being bitten by bugs and trying not to breathe through my nose! Nevertheless I would have given my kingdom for a fully operational motorbike! Al tried to send a SPOT OK message but it wasn't clear if it had worked. I fervently hoped it had, because I knew from the ferry experience that at home Helen and my family were following our movements. Whenever SPOT was making progress across the map they reasoned everything must be OK. When it stopped for too long and there was no contact from me they would worry, and Helen in particular would be frantic.

The next day we finally managed to get the bike running again. A combination of making replacement air filters from the mesh pockets of my tent and getting the carburettor cleaned and adjusted, allowed the bike to run well enough to ride to Dushanbe. This was a big relief. The bike even made it through the big scary tunnel other travellers had warned us about with fear in their voices. This tunnel was long and totally unlit. The road surface was actually dirt, made into huge ruts by the trucks. The ruts were full of water which hid large rocks. All of this was made even more hazardous by a herd of cows which had taken up residence in the tunnel and were either forming a slalom course by lying down, or even worse, haphazardly wandering about. The situation did not improve for me when, mid-tunnel, the bikes throttle stuck wide open. Thankfully I avoided crashing and managed to free it off again. All that remained was to ride the remaining distance to Dushanbe.

Although this was steeply downhill most of the way on a rocky gravel road, this would not normally have caused too much of an issue. Trouble was, during the process of swapping the carburettor and other parts; I had removed the bolt securing the rear brake fluid reservoir to move it out of the way for access. I forgot to reattach it for one particular test run and it had touched the hot exhaust so had melted, resulting in a hole. The fluid had gushed out leaving me with no rear brake. I tried in vain to re-melt the plastic with a flame and re-form it, but all attempts to repair the damage failed. Although I managed to make the cylinder hold brake fluid and could bleed the system, once under use the brake would lose pressure and fail. Riding around this little fact on this particular road was heart-stopping to say the least. Just as the road was improving and flattening on the approach into civilization, there was a final sting in the tail. All of the many test runs with a badly running bike while trying to fix it had used a lot of fuel- in fact, all of it. I ran out. Fortunately the spare can I was carrying was full, so I was able to tip in the spare five litres and carry on. This was the only time on the trip I actually ran out, and the spare fuel wasn't needed often at all.

In Dushanbe we found an expensive, one hundred dollar per night guesthouse. Unfortunately the one we were looking for was just out of sight. Dushanbe is the capital and largest city of Tajikistan. Dushanbe means "Monday" in the Tajik language. It was so named because it grew from a village that originally had a popular market on Mondays. Until 1929, the city was known in Russian as Dyushambe, and from 1929 to 1961 as Stalinabad. [xxi] We didn't see much of the place or the people though, as having slept and stocked up on provisions it was off on an easy ride to Kulob. Kulob is a city in Kulob district, Khatlon Province, Tajikistan. Located 203 km south-east of the capital Dushanbe on the Yakhsu River (a right tributary of Panj), it is one of the largest cities in the country with a population around 150,000.[xxii] We chose a southerly route. Others had warned us that the northern road may be closed. Worse than that according to some it was a 'sniper alley' and very dangerous. I felt it wasn't a good day for being shot at because I found out I had become an uncle for the first time! I'm not sure that the chicken stew for dinner was an appropriate celebration for welcoming little Darcy Jane into the world, but I'm sure she would grow up appreciating Uncle Dave's token gesture all the same. The lack of a rear brake was still annoying me, but one thing I could do was change tyres from the road biased ones I had been using to road legal, but much more off road suitable ones I had been carrying with me.

The next day I set off for Kalaichum with my new tyres in place. Kalaichum - meaning fortress on the banks of the river of Khumb, is a small town located in the Gorno-Badakhshan Autonomous Province in Tajikistan on the border with Afghanistan. Formerly it was the capital of the independent statelet of Darvaz. Now it is the capital of the Darvoz District of Tajikistan. Here the Pamir Highway meets the Panj River.

The village is an important overnight rest stop between Kulob and Khorugh, located at a distance of 168 km from Kulob (or 368 km from Dushanbe) and 235 km from Khorugh. It has several hostels to accommodate travellers on their way between cities. The village is almost entirely surrounded by the Pamir Mountains.[xxiii] We had no map of this area though so had to find the right road by asking several people, taking the most common answer as the truth! The road quickly became a stony track and we were repeatedly stopped at check points between regions, but there was no problem once they spotted the GPAO permit in our passports. This is additional to a visa and a unique requirement for Tajikistan on our route. The reasons for this type of restriction got ever more obvious. We had arrived at the part of the road which follows a river, which is the border with Afghanistan! The US led occupation of Afghanistan started back in 2001, but there were still Taliban attacks and other unrest widespread in the country. In parts the river wasn't very wide and I could have easily thrown a stone over. The road was very rough and rocky, causing us to move slowly. It was along this road that we ran into two sets of young soldiers wearing camouflage fatigues and carrying guns. They took our passports then demanded money for returning them. This lot knew they had all the power in this situation. The first set of troops were particularly aggressive, trying to open all of the pockets on my motorcycle clothes to find money or a wallet. Eventually we were forced to give them a ten note of the local currency each, which was a significant amount. At this point we didn't know whether they would really harm us or not. There were no witnesses; we were in a lawless region with a cliff on one side and a river on the other. Riding quickly or turning around was impossible on the rough terrain. I remember no panic, but there's no doubt that if you disappeared here you might never be found, and the people responsible never caught. Only afterwards did I wonder why they negotiated at all, they could have easily taken anything and everything they wanted. The second lot of soldiers were not so pushy and having survived the first round we claimed lack of money and only had to relinquish a tin of food for each of them from each of us. As this was packed on top of our loads it was an obvious target. After the second daylight robbery of the day in quick succession we made a decision. No stopping. If any more group of soldiers came along and signalled for us to stop we would give a friendly wave back as if not understanding their signals and open the throttles and blast past as fast as possible. We would end up with nothing left if this continued all day! It worked. More troops came, but none stood right in front as the first group had and we rode past at the limits of our off road speed, not daring to look back.

Where we found anyone who had an understanding of English we would ask about the road conditions. They were generally bad but one helpful chap, having seen our exotic bikes, had coined the phrase "Easy for Moto!" From then on this phrase was used as a rallying cry whenever the going looked to be getting rough. It definitely applied to a very dodgy looking bridge we came across. Then there was our first serious river crossing. The fast flowing water over a foot deep in places and threatened to soak everything should we make a mistake. My boots had completely lost any semblance of waterproofing by this stage and my feet were regularly soaked, especially if I lost momentum and had to put a steadying foot into the freezing water. At one stage we rode through a waterfall, cascading down a cliff and over the road. This type of thing showed clearly how the mudslide had been caused which formed the latest block on our progress. We had to wait a half hour or so while the mudslide was cleared. Then they cleared a path of sorts with a bulldozer but there was not a recognisable road surface. It was just a very uneven mound of loose earth, mud and rocks. We went for it up the steep slope, inching past trucks as we went. Al dropped his bike once here, but unusually I managed not to. The road improved and we made it to "town". It was a sleepy little place and we had been told to register with the local police when in town in these parts. We found the small police station on the main, perhaps only, street through town and registered without any issues. Petrol stations in the conventional sense of the word had become a rarity. Although nervous about the quality of the fuel there was no choice but to get petrol pumped out from big barrel at the side of the road. We found a guesthouse by asking around, which was much more basic than those which had come before. On arrival we were invited to lounge on a large platform outside, while they brought us bread and a drink. Not being very physically flexible myself and unused to not having a proper chair, this was pretty uncomfortable! On the other hand this place really looked like what I imagined rural accommodation to be in far off lands. Chickens clucked around the grass and bushes. Only the occasional dog barking interrupted the tranquillity of the sunlight streaming through the rustling trees. Our dinner that night appeared to be largely chicken skin and potato. I'm not sure if this was a local delicacy, or whether they just didn't fancy wasting their chicken meat on us. We whiled away the evening changing a tyre on Al's bike. I still had no back brake and no prospect of getting it fixed. To be honest a bike which didn't stop didn't concern me nearly as much as one which didn't go. The house seemed to be two rooms total. One room was vacated for us so presumably the family had to get pretty cosy when guests arrived. We slept on carpets on the floor with lots of flies for company. Despite that, sleep came fairly easily after such a crazy day.

On the hard floor the sleep didn't last though, so we were up early and on the road to Chorug at 06:30. We made good progress and ignored the border patrol "kids with guns". There was at least one for every hut where we would have to have our passports checked. It was another day of drama on the road. First came a river crossing where I went too fast, keen not to get stuck in the middle and water got drawn into the engine making it stall. Thankfully it restarted and I revved it hard to clear the water out the exhaust. Next we ran into a major mudslide blocking the road. Most of the people present were more interested in looking on lazily than helping. We helped get two cars across then dug a path for our bikes. A few of the onlookers got into the spirit and we managed to manhandle the bikes across with their help. The rest of the journey that day was a blast over tarmac and gravel roads with my bike running well. We were aiming for a place called the Pamir Lodge which we had heard recommended on the internet, and found it with some difficulty. It was floor style sleeping again but a lot more commercial, hence there were some backpackers staying. The scenery had been pretty stunning today and put me in mind of a bigger, badder lake district. There were lots of smiles and waves again as we passed and it was nice to share these experiences while relaxing and chatting with the backpackers.

We were getting into the really high country of the Pamir Mountains now but it presented no problems for me or the bike! We blasted all the way to Murgog, about 200 miles over mainly tarmac and some gravel covered roads. In the morning we came across a small market and picked up fresh eggs and round unleavened bread. I carried the eggs as gently as I could in my motorcycle jacket pockets, knowing for sure that anywhere else on the bike they could be shattered in seconds. I hoped they wouldn't make a mess and was relieved to find them still in one piece when we found a place to pull over for breakfast in a wide valley with a shallow river running through it. We scrambled the eggs on our petrol stove and used the bread to wrap them and stuff them into our faces. In this amazing scenery, in an adventure and extra hungry the *very* free range eggs and freshly baked local bread tasted incredible.

While fantastically fresh that day, we later found to our cost that the bread, devoid of all the nasty extra ingredients found in supermarket bread, went stale and rock hard very quickly. This felt like a blow because we couldn't guarantee to come across a similar market at a convenient time each day! The spectacular scenery continued all the way through the Pamirs. We travelled past awe inspiring huge mountains with snow-capped peaks, and over a mountain pass at fourteen thousand feet high!

Getting towards our evening stopover we bumped into Tiffany Coates and her friend. We had known that they were also travelling roughly in this direction at the same time via Horizons Unlimited. Tiffany and her BMW motorcycle are something of legends of overlanding, having already travelled through many countries on different continents. She seems to have developed an affinity for her bike that I certainly wasn't building up with mine, given the long list of "features" it had developed. We teamed up and I noted with interest that her technique for bargaining on price was much more finely honed than either of ours. We benefitted from the reduced rate by staying in same place. Finding petrol in this town wasn't straightforward. We started by asking the owner of the guesthouse. He responded by getting on the phone, and after a short conversation motioned us to follow his car. He led us up a winding dirt track past various buildings to a gate. Here a four wheel drive vehicle with barrels on it filled up our bikes. One could never find this without help, and the guys were all very jovial. This could well be because they were charging us the "tourist rate", but cynicism aside this was a remote area and unless you wanted to push your bike, any fuel was good value!

Tiffany volunteered to cook an evening meal of vegetable curry if we would ride off to a nearby market and pick up some ingredients. This seemed like a good deal and the market, although a scruffy looking patch of ground surrounded by metal containers looked unpromising, it had sufficient variety of fresh produce for our needs. Just as importantly, in one dimly lit container one of the traders had vodka for sale. The Russian influence through this region means that vodka is sold in half litre bottles. Although these are smaller than the standard at home there is a reason for that. Once opened in the hands of a local a bottle is never closed. In fact, the bottle caps are of such poor quality that it is almost impossible to close a bottle once it is open. Whether the poor quality caps or the appetite to finish a bottle came first wasn't clear. Back at the guesthouse ingredients were turned into excellent curry using Tiffany's supply of spices. I helped out by chopping the vegetables. There was no mobile signal here and high in the mountains it felt very remote. Al was suffering from headaches brought on by the altitude. Despite the altitude, and the vodka, I felt good.

Kyrgyzstan

The night at altitude was cold. The next day was supposed to be our last full day in Tajikistan and a short riding day to the big lake not far from the Kyrgyzstan border. The road was good tarmac mostly, but we failed to pick up any supplies as the bazaar was shut in the morning. When we arrived at the lake it seemed very high up in the mountains still and very inhospitable. We had not come down much since passing over the highest pass we would see, fifteen thousand and thirty feet above sea level. There was a town of sorts on the lake edge, but it looked for all the world like a ghost town. There was no sign of life at all. Getting hungry, we stopped at the side of the road and clambered down the incline for shelter from the wind, leaving the bikes on the road edge. We cooked noodles and were just having our lunch when several Brits turned up on their huge BMW GS's. These guys were all on the UKGSers forum and were on their way back from Mongolia. They had gone the fast way through Russia and were keeping up an even more furious pace than us. From the UK all the way to the Mongolian capital had taken them something like only seventeen days. We had a good chat with them and they let us know that the border ahead was friendly and a few good places to stay as well. Nothing they said put us off so we headed on to Kyrgyzstan. As promised the border was no problem. There was a big no man's land between the two border outposts, and there was nothing there but some Swiss cyclists coming the other way. Crossing the border we came into a new mobile phone network area and fifteen messages all turned up at once. This was pretty frustrating but at least I got these communications from the last several days eventually. Kyrgyzstan instantly seemed less harsh. Although we hadn't expected to see them until Mongolia there were "Gers" or "Yurts" all down the green valley that the road wound down through.

These are traditional round Mongolian tents where whole families live, able to move their whole community with the seasons. The road was like the Stelvio Pass in Italy but recreated in mud form! The people here began to look a lot more Mongolian also. We eventually found a rough camp site far enough from other residents to not cause too much interest. On top of a cliff overlooking the river in the bottom of the valley where smoke rose slowly from the Gers below. Again the scenery reminded me of the Lake District, and in these pleasant surroundings we had a great dinner of pasta washed down with vodka. I marvelled at just how far we had come. At one point today we could see over the border fence and into China from the road. It was very tempting to nip through a hole in the fence and take a walk in China, especially as it wasn't on our route. However it felt like there could always be a border guard watching over these sensitive border regions and common sense prevailed. The bike needed some attention again, because the number plate had fallen off and the engine needed more oil. I hoped to pick up some more in Osh, the next large town and created a replacement number plate using card, a pen and document wallet to keep it dry. I ended the day very tired indeed.

The odometer clicked over seven thousand seven hundred miles during an easy morning heading down to Osh. Osh is the second largest city in Kyrgyzstan, located in the Fergana Valley in the south of the country and often referred to as the "capital of the south". The city is the most ancient in all of Kyrgyzstan at least 3,000 years old, and has served as the administrative centre of Osh Province since 1939. The city has an ethnically mixed population of about 250,000, comprising Kyrgyz, Uzbeks, Russians, Tajiks, and other smaller ethnic groups.[xxiv]

The long range fuel tank on my bike came into its own here giving two hundred and sixty miles on one tank to get there without running dry. We changed money then bought food, petrol and oil. The main road into Osh was lined with shacks selling products for cars, including the oil I needed. This was another pretty odd stroke of luck. I've never seen another street like that before or since. We got lost navigating out of this built up area and on to the right road which frustratingly wasted two hours. It had become very hot again and the bike stopped couple of times. Closer inspection revealed that heat was indeed the problem. The bike was overheating because of lack of oil and the ambient temperature. At this stage I wasn't sure whether all the oil was being burned by the engine or if some was just leaking out somewhere. I put in about two litres of fresh oil and hoped fervently that it hadn't done lasting damage to the engine. Cars passed with a toot and a wave and when we stopped nervous kids would sidle up to us as their curiosity got the better of their shyness. I gave them some sweets and chocolates. My bike was looking pretty rough by now, not helped by my new home-made cardboard number plate. I wasn't sure if anyone would care, or even notice the lack of a number plate here, but thought that if the number on the bike matched the ownership documentation this might help at borders, even if the plate was home-made! It was wild camping again that evening. Our dinner of spicy pasta was very good. While shopping for supplies we had noticed a strange phenomenon. Some bottles of wine here seemed to be promoted by big Hollywood stars! We purchased a bottle of red wine with a picture of Angelina Jolie plastered over it. On drinking it I'm sure she would not have approved.

The wine was sickly sweet and not very nice at all! We were wild camping and as the evening drew to a close it became quite stormy, thunder and lightning with heavy rain. In my tent my mind could wander to random thoughts, like 'the hats they wear in this country are very cool!' Or even, 'I really stink'.

The next day we were charging up a mountainside towards the big pass of the day. Trying to set off again after a photo stop, the bike toppled over on the rough ground. Petrol started pouring from the carburettor. I turned the fuel taps off at the petrol tank and started the now familiar trouble shooting process. In this instance we ended up taking the carburettor out of the bike and completely dismantling it at side of road.

I had with me a bright orange survival bag designed to crawl into if one is caught out and exposed overnight in bad weather. This served as the workbench for the operation, helping to avoid losing any of the tiny parts. The internals of the carburettor had become dirty because of home-made air filters. These were letting enough air in, but were letting in other particles too. Not a good situation. The bike was still in need of more oil. While it was running OK I knew this wasn't good for the long term. I had gradually come to the realisation that grit getting through the air filters and into the engine must have scored the piston barrel in the engine. This would mean major surgery if the bike was to keep going indefinitely. Our next opportunity to get some mechanical help would be in Almaty. It was a hard days riding, off road all the way. Considering the state of the bike I was hoping to hit tarmac soon, as dirt would end up getting past the air filters. It also felt much easier on the bike in general. We had a lunch of the now familiar noodles by an idyllic winding river. Later in the day we rounded the crest of a hill and came out on most amazing view. I had never seen anything like it. The sunlight seemed to cast deep shadows on the bumpy foothills then brilliantly reflect off the snow-capped mountains in the distance. To complete the scene a young lad on his horse came galloping up to us, and followed alongside our bikes for a short distance. We found a wild camping spot, but it was quite exposed. A major storm blew through with gale force winds threatening to tear the tent pegs from the ground. In time the storm passed and the winds died as quickly as they had begun, leaving a peaceful night.

We left about nine in the morning after trying to improve the home-made air filter set-up on my bike. It was a relief to make it to a tarmac road. The bike broke down, but being much more familiar with the problem a lack of air was quickly diagnosed. The new filter set-up was too restrictive for the day's high altitude, around ten thousand feet above sea level, so I had to put it back to the previous set-up. The problem of particles getting through the mesh was compounded by the bike occasionally backfiring through the carburettor when I shut the throttle and blowing a big hole in the delicate filter. The bike was now drinking a huge amount of oil, one litre per hundred miles. There was no real other option than carrying on towards the border and to Almaty in Kazakhstan for repairs, 300 miles or so away. We rode past Lake Karakul which was large but not nearly as spectacular as others we'd seen. It is also known as Issyk Kul and is in the northern Tian Shan mountains in eastern Kyrgyzstan. It is the tenth largest lake in the world by volume and the second largest saline lake after the Caspian Sea. Although it is surrounded by snow-capped peaks, supposedly it never freezes, hence its name, which means "hot lake" in the Kyrgyz language.

The lake is a Ramsar site of globally significant biodiversity and forms part of the Issyk-Kul Biosphere Reserve. It was the site of an ancient metropolis 2,500 years ago, and archaeological excavations are ongoing.[xxv] There were more police in this part of Kyrgyzstan than elsewhere, but they didn't give us any trouble. Our route took us through a nature reserve which cost one thousand "summi" to get into, but where we were rewarded with scenery that got ever more green and lush. I was loving being able just to cruise along the smooth tarmac. It made a nice change from the concentration and physical effort that all the off road riding demanded.

We had found a type of cooked tinned beef for sale in these parts and used it to make sandwiches for lunch. The beef tasted surprisingly good. Later we ate more pasta for dinner with a bottle of wine each. The alcohol consumption felt deserved after a day's riding and seemed to keep a lid on the increasingly strained relations between Al and me. The continued issues with my bike were the biggest problem, but it was getting blamed personally which I felt was unfair. It irritated me that that there appeared to be an attitude that if there was a problem with his bike, it was all part of the adventure, but a problem with my bike was the biggest inconvenience in the world. There's no doubt the bike could have been better prepared, but I was no mechanic, and the professionals I had got involved only made things worse! There was nothing to suggest so many problems when I bought the machine. Al had even said that if I didn't buy that one he would have. Our wild camp last night was well away from main road. In good spirits from the wine we messed about throwing stones, which were scattered everywhere on the ground, at a target. I christened the game "Rocky Throw Throw" as it brought to mind some crazy Japanese game shows I had seen on TV on a previous holiday in Japan. The weather closed in bringing more cloud and rain during the night.

Kazakhstan

Leaving Lake Karakul after blasting along the lake edge, it took an age to find food in Karakul itself. We tried to recreate the magic of the previous scrambled egg butty for lunch, but I don't think it could ever quite match up! Each time we stopped I would also top up the engine oil. The ground had flattened out and we crossed a grassy plain to the border. It rapidly became clear that getting out of Kyrgyzstan wouldn't be so easy. On the way into the country Al had merrily waltzed past customs and straight through the unguarded gateway into the country proper. I'd suggested that we must have missed something because we had only done two of the holy trinity of border crossing, Passport Control, Immigration, Customs. As a result we had no customs declaration. We were called into the office of the chief customs official. He spoke English quite well. After he explained to us that we had made a grave mistake and would have to go all the way back to our entry point, I knew we would have to make some kind of deal. I asked how we might be able to solve the problem here. This seemed to strike the right chord with our guy. He asked us if we were carrying any knives. It was an unusual question and the way he asked didn't suggest that it would be a problem if we were. Al produced his multi-tool which the customs official inspected, but seemed unimpressed. I pulled out a silver Swiss army style knife Helen had bought for me for the trip. This seemed much more to his liking and he queried "Is this a present for me?" Yes I replied, warming to the game of bribery without anyone saying the words. That was all it took, no money changed hands and our customs problem was resolved. Knives seemed to be a hot property at this border because the passport control guard wanted a knife too. However, I wasn't running a knife shop and our passports, unlike our customs declaration, were in order so I ignored his request and he went home empty handed. Entry into Kazakhstan was easy. This time we made sure to ask for a customs declaration. Warm weather and a tarmac road made for a nice start to Kazakhstan. Searching for a camp site we veered off the main road and down a dirt track into a canyon with a river running through it. This seemed to be a well-used weekend camping spot as there were the remains of numerous open fires and a fair quantity of empty vodka bottles. We were only about a hundred and twenty miles from Almaty and hopefully a motorcycle garage, where I hoped they would be able to mend my troubled bike. I managed to get data service on my mobile here by climbing back up the steep cliff to the higher ground near the road. The road passed over the canyon where our camp was set up via a suspension bridge. The evening took on the familiar routine of wine and spicy pasta, although that night's version was weirdly very salty! It was odd to think that after Kazakhstan there were only two countries left to make it through to my main target of Ulaanbaatar, but in terms of miles there was still such a long way to go.

It was an easy tarmac ride to Almaty, over eight thousand four hundred miles since leaving home. Almaty is the largest city in Kazakhstan, and was the country's capital until 1997. Despite losing its status as the capital to Astana, Almaty remains the major commercial and cultural centre of Kazakhstan, as well as its largest population centre. The city is located in the mountainous area of southern Kazakhstan.[xxvi] The traffic became heavier and heavier. We found an internet café and looked up a hotel. Hotel Kasshol was sixty thousand Tenge, or around three hundred pounds for four nights. Despite being expensive the hotel WIFI was extra. I paid the whole bill on my credit card which was the first time I'd used it, preferring to use cash where possible to avoid any possible fraud attempts. Getting cash was in itself tricky though. The first cash machine I found seemed to work fine, but gave me no money at the end of the transaction! I just had to hope that it hadn't subtracted the money from my account. The next machine gave me about fifty pounds, which I then immediately spent on lunch. Almaty was proving to be pricey! Eventually another machine relinquished a hundred pounds to keep me going. It was quite amazing to be in civilization after all of the wild camping. There was pleasure in the simple things, like having a shower and getting properly clean! We made plans to get my bike to a garage tomorrow, hoping that it would be open on a Sunday.

After a decent breakfast in the hotel we went off to find "My Town Motos". This garage had come recommended on the internet, although as far as we could tell there was little alternative. The web had provided us with GPS coordinates which took us close, but we had to flag down another biker to actually find it. When we got there another young lad was waiting for them to open. He spoke good English and translated for us which was very handy. Although I felt sure of what the answer would be, I felt I had no alternative but to let them open the engine to fault find. This would cost two hundred dollars and it was unlikely to mend the problem as there were no spares to fix anything on our bikes here. We were told nowhere in Kazakhstan would have spares and that Russia would be our best hope.

Leaving the bike at the garage I had a pillion ride back to the centre of town. We had lunch at City Café, which became a favourite spot on the corner of a main pedestrian street. This was a place to see and be seen, and the sights on this street were incredible. The fashionable young women of Almaty seemed to compete for attention. Many seemed to have a mixed ethnicity, part Russian but with softer eastern features which made them very striking. Bumming around Almaty we checked out a dodgy looking market and then got the cable car up the mountain which overlooks the city and provides a nice view from the top. Not having to cook over the camp stove, we ended up with an average dinner for an above average price, and then had a couple of beers at the obligatory Irish bar. The entertainment here was both free and uninvited! A local woman, probably in her forties and clearly very drunk sat down at our table and proceeded to explain that it was the anniversary of her husband's death and that she was very upset. The story of her life got more and more elaborate as she explained in good English that she had been a dancer and choreographer. Al was ignoring her entirely, but I couldn't help but respond as it seemed so rude not to. Her performance reached a dramatic climax as she openly mocked Al's dirty shirt to his face, then asked if I would go back to her home and have sex with her. It was time for a quick getaway and I was still chuckling as an old woman we were passing in the street let out an enormous fart. It might be pretty basic as humour goes, but this was easily the funniest part of the trip since inventing "Rocky Throw Throw".

Without a bike to ride and a direction to ride in, life in Almaty was a bit aimless. I updated my blog and sat in the park, then wandered the city looking for a barber, but to no avail. Later we went back to "My Town Motos" to find the bike in pieces. After a long conversation translated by phone, we established that the bike needed a new piston and re-bore of the cylinder, much as expected. The garage agreed to put it back together having smoothed the crank. All we could do was get on the internet and look to have parts shipped to us in Russia from the UK. I rang Wemoto about sending a piston kit to Russia as they appeared to have it in stock. So far it had cost around three hundred dollars in labour and one hundred and seventy pounds for the kit from Wemoto, without delivery! I was glad to find that when I took the battery out of the battery box the two hundred dollars I had taped in there for emergencies was still safe and sound. I'd forgotten to remove this money before leaving the bike with the garage. On leaving however, our good fortune was reversed. Al's Garmin navigation unit was stolen in broad daylight right outside the garage while we were inside. As he was also feeling ill, it was not a happy camp. The pillion rides to and from the garage got easier as I got used to not being in control and the lack of any passenger foot pegs on Al's bike. These had been removed to fit the pannier rack. There were thunder storms in the sky as I tucked into a tasty chicken curry at Mad Murphy's, the aforementioned Irish bar. After hunting around town, on returning to the hotel I found out there was a barber shop in the basement! My need for a haircut wasn't quite fulfilled though, the door was firmly closed.

Al was visibly annoyed at the loss of his GPS device, and even though I didn't find it particularly useful I offered to pay half for a replacement. I knew I'd not see any value from this investment except perhaps a less grumpy travelling companion! A day passed doing mundane things; even having a shave was a big deal. I had been cultivating a bearded look while on the road in contrast to my usual clean cut persona. I tried cash machines whenever I passed one and frequented Mad Murphy's for their lunchtime bacon and egg sandwiches. There was a frustrating trip over to "My Town Moto" to try and get my bike back, only to find that they had not finished putting it back together. Our hotel was full, so staying an extra night we were told could be a problem. In the evening we returned to City Café for kebab sandwiches and beer while watching the world go by. I finally got my bike back and the garage had not even been able to find any new air filters to fit. I just had to hope that it would last to Ulaanbaatar. In the end the hotel managed to squeeze us in for an extra night, which was good news. We made preparations to depart, getting fuel, oil and food, but it all felt a bit lazy and disorganised.

On day fifty five after leaving home we got up and left Almaty. We just took on a relatively short ride to a reservoir which we thought would be good for camping. We changed to suitable tyres again amid a huge thunderstorm. In the process Al punctured my front inner tube and broke off a bolt on my front wheel. All this after lecturing me on not forcing it! Our tyre choices were causing more need for change overs than should have been the case. Not only that, but we still weren't very good at it. It wouldn't be until later in the trip that I learned a better technique from a local, after which it was easy. Anyway, it was good to be back riding and camping. Camp dinners hadn't changed much; pasta with tuna, sweetcorn and sauce and a bottle of crap wine each. I re-bodged my air filters and crossed my fingers for the umpteenth time that it would work. Not that if it did the oil consumption would decrease. There was plenty of dry wood around and we had going the best camp fire of the trip so far. It was a shame there was nothing to cook over the flames. I hoped that we could get some good miles in the following day. I wanted to get to Russia and feel like we were progressing. I heard from home that my cousin Gemma who lives in China had given birth for the first time. At this stage I wasn't to know just how soon I would get to see the new baby. Camping out it was good to hear the crickets again after the usual city noises of the past few days. Stranded in Almaty I was beginning to wonder why I was out there, but being on the road helped me to remember.

After eggs for breakfast we got quite a few more miles in. Long straight roads meant two hundred miles was less of a problem, although we got soaked in a thunder storm again. The highlight was seeing an old Russian missile base. The concrete bunkers were huge and camouflaged from the air by having been covered in earth with grass allowed to grow on top. Russian made fighter jets tore through the sky above us as the Kazakh air force completed training manoeuvres. This point on the journey had me thinking hard about how it would end. Only thoughts of what I would get to see and experience in Russia and Mongolia made me want to keep going. I wasn't at all sure how to broach the idea that had formed in my mind. I didn't want to ship my dying the bike out of the far side of Russia to the USA via Korea as planned. There were a few different reasons. First and foremost I didn't want to follow Al around the states maintaining the status quo. His moods and temper tantrums were becoming more and more absurd and frequent and I was tired of walking on egg shells. I knew that I could easily be independent there, with no need for the shared plans and equipment that kept us together. The bike had been so used and abused it was now more or less worthless and fixing it up well enough to perform adequately in a first world country with lots of traffic and high speed roads would be expensive. Shipping itself we had estimated to cost around four thousand pounds, which seemed insane for a worthless bike. Even buying again elsewhere would be a better option. Finally I was running out of time. We had agreed to a schedule that we clearly weren't going to keep. While a few days extra meant nothing to Al, who seemingly had no real ties back at home, it was important to me. One of the things I had agreed with Helen was to meet her in the USA for a holiday in the middle of the trip. This meant we would not have to be apart for so long and was important for our relationship. I needed to find out if I could leave the bike in Mongolia or Russia. We would be in Russia twice on the planned route. Leaving during the first Russia leg would mean I would miss Mongolia which I really didn't want to do, so that didn't seem like a good option. On the other hand I felt that I'd happily call Ulaanbaatar the end of this leg of the trip and part ways. I didn't want to go home; I just didn't want to take any more of this mental torment past the point where I had achieved my goals.

A whole day of flat featureless plains saw us race past nine thousand one hundred miles and end in the unpromising town of Semey. Semey, formerly known as Semipalatinsk, is a city in the north-eastern province of East Kazakhstan, and in the Kazakhstan part of Siberia, near the border with Russian Federation, around 1,000 kilometres north of Almaty, and 700 kilometres southeast of the Russian city of Omsk, along the Irtysh River. [xxvii] We searched around for a hotel and spotted a large sign. Riding around the back to the entrance revealed that the gates were locked and there seemed to be nobody around. Pressing an intercom button resulted in a cleaner coming to see what we wanted. She didn't let us in, but got on the phone and soon a car arrived. Hotel Rich turned out to be owned by Igor. He was a stocky intimidating man with a bald head. He spoke next to no English either, but managed to indicate we could stay and suggested a price. We indicated that it was a bit expensive for us and he reduced it down to a level we were more comfortable with. He opened up what appeared to be a private garage in which we could park our bikes. I began to wonder what sort of a hotel is all locked up, has a private garage, and appears to have no other guests. In the garage was Igor's own motorbike, a BMW HP2 Supermoto. This is an expensive bike, but Igor knew how to use it. He promptly started it up, and in a flurry of revs tore out of the garage and out of the hotel grounds to reappear on the main road passing the side of the hotel above us. He then proceeded to pull enormous wheelies up and down this public road wearing no helmet or protective gear at all for about five minutes. It was surreal, that in a place of this size we had rolled quite by accident into the hotel of a biking nutcase.

The hotel was spacious and new throughout, but was laid out more like a house and private clubhouse than a hotel. We were shown to a vast twin room with private en-suite bathroom. The furnishing was plain, but there was no doubting the specification of the new western style bathroom. After a while Igor left, leaving us with a girl whom at first I thought might be the hotel's receptionist. Julia was tall and slim and wore high platform sandals. She obviously didn't speak any English either, but as there was a computer she had the idea to go to a translation website and type in phrases before clicking translate. In this way we could slowly communicate back and forth. Apparently Julia didn't work there but was helping out. Something about Igor's familiarity with her made us ask whether she was his girlfriend, although there was clearly at least a twenty year age gap. She insisted she was not.

Later on Igor reappeared having rounded up a few friends. We were to join them for dinner. Upstairs in the "hotel" was a large room containing a full size snooker table, a lounge area with television and a bar. Evidently this was a party in our honour! One of the friends spoke better English and I discovered he was some sort of motocross star, we were shown lots of photographs of him in action. The other friend, we were told, was the local police chief. This was getting really weird! Igor ordered food and in due course a delivery arrived. We had pizza, chicken and another dish I had never seen before. I asked what it was called in Russian, but the only name they gave me was "double pizza". It was easy to see why, it was large and round like a pizza, with another pizza upturned on the top so that the toppings were in the middle and crusts top and bottom. However somehow it wasn't heavy, it was light and delicious. The beer and vodka also flowed and after a while Al went off to bed. I foolishly stayed up drinking shots of vodka with these crazy Kazakhs until I was very, very drunk! I felt increasingly like the empty hotel must be a front for some sort of organised crime ring, with the chief of police on the payroll and the local sports star seduced by the money and lifestyle, and with Igor as the Kingpin. The drink had put everyone in high spirits and the plot thickened when Igor took out his phone, leant over and turned the screen to me. He then flipped through several photographs of a young woman on a bed in compromising poses wearing revealing red underwear. It was Julia. Mafia bosses plaything perhaps?

I eventually staggered off towards bed, but ended up in the bathroom vomiting numerous times. My vodka skills were no match for these guys! In the morning an omelette and coffee made by the mysterious Julia helped me to recover. However the hangovers were such that any thoughts of continuing on the bikes today as planned were thrown out. It was fortunate as Igor seemed keen for us to stay. He managed to communicate that we would go out for a picnic. Igor's friends had rounded up their families and, in three four wheel drive vehicles, all of us set off out of town and into the countryside. We pulled off the main road and down a tight, rutted dirt track through trees. At this point I was still a little nervous that we were willingly being taken to a secluded spot to be killed for daring to turn up at their hotel. Only two things kept me from panicking in my hangover haze. First the thought that if they wanted to kill us then last night would have been just as easy, and second that they had brought their children along in the cars! Igor did nothing to calm my imagination when we stopped at a picturesque spot on a river bank. From the boot of the car he produced a petrol driven chainsaw and an axe. Thankfully the point of these became quickly evident as Igor cut a large branch from a nearby tree and chopped it into smaller pieces to make a fire. The wives had set up a table on which they were spreading all kinds of food. The fire was lit and once it died down, chicken breast was barbequed over the glowing embers. There was one more surprise in store. Igor pulled a large box from the back of his car and attached what was inside to an electric pump plugged into the car. As it inflated a small boat took shape! It was completed by attaching a small outboard motor and launched into the river. I was offered a try and splodged into the river and jumped aboard. I motored around on the river for a short time, the current was quite strong. With the current the boat would go quite fast but against it hardly move at all. I pushed the thought that this area had been a Russian nuclear testing ground during the cold war to the back of my mind, and hoped that messing about in the river wouldn't do me any harm! In 1949, a site on the steppe 150 km west of the city was chosen by the Soviet atomic bomb programme to be the location for its weapons testing. For decades, Kurchatov (the secret city at the heart of the test range named for Igor Kurchatov, father of the Soviet atomic bomb) was home to many of the brightest stars of Soviet weapons science. The Soviet Union operated the Semipalatinsk Test Site from the first explosion in 1949 until 1989; 456 nuclear tests, including 340 underground and 116 atmospheric tests, were conducted there.

Semey has suffered serious environmental and health effects from the time of its atomic prosperity: nuclear fallout from the atmospheric tests and uncontrolled exposure of the workers, most of whom lived in the city, have given Semey and neighbouring villages high rates of cancer, childhood leukaemia, impotence and birth defects.[xxviii]

Russia

The next day we left the very amazing hospitality behind and escaped Igor's world intact. It was seventy five easy miles ride to the border, but when we got there it was one of the slowest yet. We had just bought insurance when another Brit called Dave rolled up on his XT660. This is the next generation model bike to the ones we were riding. It took about three and a half hours to get out of Kazakhstan and into Russia. Although it was longwinded, it was also corruption free. It didn't help us that we also lost an hour time difference at this crossing which made us six hours ahead of UK. We rode on together with Dave a while further then camped up at the edge of a farmer's field. Two cars passed along the dirt track we had used to get away from the main road. The occupants of both cars seemed happy to see us. One of the cars stopped and without a word of shared language they handed us a loaf of locally made bread. Gestures of kindness such as this never failed to leave me dumbstruck at the human spirit normal people throughout the world possess. It also made me consider if I would take the time to help a visitor to the UK with the same level of generosity. The mosquitoes at this camp spot were pretty bad so we rushed to prepare a dinner of cow, pasta and rice. We had taken to calling the tinned beef, "cow" because the pictures of cows on the label were the only way we could guess at the contents of the tin when we were buying it. My bike was still suffering from burning oil and an irritating throttle problem. Sometimes, even with the throttle firmly shut the engine would race away to two thousand revolutions per minute. I felt good regardless though, it was nice to have some different company and we had made it into Russia!

The following day we headed towards the Russian city of Barnaul. Barnaul was founded in 1730. Originally chosen for its proximity to the mineral-rich Altai Mountains and its location on a major river, the site was founded by the wealthy Demidov family in the 1730s. In addition to the copper which had originally attracted the Demidovs, substantial deposits of silver were soon found as well. In 1747, the Demidovs' factories were taken over by the Crown, and soon became the major silver centre of Russia. By the 1900s, Barnaul had grown into a major centre of trade and culture of the region, especially after the construction of the Turkestan-Siberia Railway. In 1914, Barnaul was the site of a draft riot, Russia's largest during World War I, which resulted in over a hundred casualties. Although the city was thousands of miles away from the actual fighting, hundreds of thousands of citizens from Altai Krai fought and died at the front in the course of the Second World War too, a fact commemorated by a large memorial in central Barnaul.[xxix]

Dave had got in touch with a local biker group and when he called, one of them rode out in our direction to find us. He led us into the city and to a reasonable hotel. Barnaul is not a pretty city. During the evening I checked my phone messages and found out that the father of a good friend of mine at home had died suddenly. I called Jonathan as soon as I heard to offer my condolences. One of the disadvantages of being away was not being able to help friends when they were in need. As far as I was concerned, riding with a third person was great, it created a different dynamic and shielded me from Al's moods and outbursts. Dave needed to stay another day in Barnaul to try and fix the rear spring on his bike. I argued that we should wait and continue to ride with him. Al wasn't having any of it; he didn't want to compromise "his" trip to fit in with what someone else might want or need. Before we left I apologised to Dave for not waiting. It was behaviour like this that was making me start to think that Alistair had only ever asked me along to help financially and perhaps to calm any fears he may have had about going it alone. I naively thought that it was going to turn into some kinds of cheesy American buddy road movie; yeah we would our ups and downs, but would come out of it the best of friends. It was shame that that didn't appear to be happening.

This next day had an odd feeling about it. Al was in a foul mood (again!) although the back pain which had been enforcing regular stops was suddenly cured enough to ride long stints. I felt that this was a lot more to do with what was going on in his head than what was going on in his back. Stopping at a roadside garage I managed to buy eight litres of oil. The bike was running OK other than leaking and burning oil and I figured that eight litres should get me all the way to the capital of Mongolia which was really the next big place, with nothing much in between. At this stage, with over 9600 miles under our belts, the grief I was getting from my companion's mood swings rose to new levels. We had been sharing resources and paying half from the start, but the garage where I bought the oil also sold groceries. While shopping Al spat angrily that he was "just buying what I want" and that he'd "rather split everything up", indicating that I should also buy food individually. Any team ethic seemed to have totally disintegrated. However by the time the evening came it was a different story. I held back fully expecting to eat the provisions I had bought when Al gave a surprised look and told me to "get stuck in, I got it for both of us". I couldn't understand the ups and downs at all, and racked my brains thinking what I might have done to trigger them. In the end I had to just try and feel better that at least for the present the mood was better. We had reached the Altay region of Russia which is quite a tourist area for the Russians themselves. The Altai Mountains are a mountain range in East-Central Asia, where Russia, China, Mongolia and Kazakhstan come together, and are where the rivers Irtysh and Ob have their headwaters. The northwest end of the range merges with the Sayan Mountains to the east, and extends southeast from there to where it gradually becomes lower and merges into the high plateau of the Gobi Desert.[xxx] The hills, trees and rivers provide a good area for adventurous outdoor activity and I saw several groups kayaking. While riding along we pulled over at a row of stalls selling the sorts of locally made souvenirs often seen in Europe. I bought some small gifts for Helen, hoping that I could carry them back without them getting broken. As the afternoon wore on we found a great camp spot. It was off the road with hills and trees around and next to a river for water. We had a decent camp fire going and cooked on it. After some wine and vodkas sleep came easily again, with dreams of Mongolia, after all at this pace there should be only one more night in Russia for us.

Our last full day in Russia was a full day of riding through great scenery. On my bike, the exhaust fell off in a comedy style at one point but no "real problems". Mongolia was a bit of an unknown, so we felt the need to stock up on supplies before the border. Last night's campsite was eclipsed by the best campsite so far, and one of the best of the whole adventure. Although deserted when we got there, it was a weekend and other car loads of people also began to arrive as it was understandably popular. I helped to push the Lada of one of the other campers back out of the wooded dirt track that he had ambitiously attempted. It was nice to help someone after all the assistance we had received on our travels. Our camp site was on another river bank, a two minute off road ride from the route we were travelling. The short grass allowed us to pitch our tents just a few yards from the shallow rivers edge. We found some wood which had been pre-cut and left by previous campers. It was dry and the fire started with a single match. This really was the place that you would envisage in your mind's eye as a campsite for a Boys' Own adventure. It could easily have been the place to shoot a film of one of the Famous Five books! I couldn't help but feel that I should have been having the time of my life. I had fuel, food, a motorcycle, water, no security worries, I didn't unduly miss home. None of these were the problem, and with someone on the same wavelength for company this would have been perfect. As I fell asleep I could still hear the dying embers of the fire popping and crackling.

Mongolia

As it turned out we had the last good campsite in the Altay. Soon after leaving in the direction of the border with Mongolia the land became barren and the lush beautiful landscape of the Altay faded. We reached the border town sooner than expected. In order to spend the last of our roubles we filled up with petrol and bought food from a small shop. In the shop the lady behind the counter seemed to try and tell us not to buy some tins with a picture of a cow on the front as we had done before. We weren't sure why so we just smiled and bought them anyway. The formalities to exit Russia were a bit tedious but OK; this border had not long been open to foreigners. Entry into Mongolia was easy and cost only forty five roubles each. The whole process was facilitated by young English speaking girls who ran the show with surprising efficiency. We were lucky however to just get through all the paperwork including buying insurance before their lunch break. As had happened before, the land somehow knew how to change at the border. It instantly looked like the Mongolia I'd seen in photographs and dreamt of riding into. We took to asking locals about the best route to take eastwards. We followed their advice not to go on the North route, as we were told the recent rains had swollen the streams and rivers enough to make them impassable. There were basically three routes across Mongolia, the North, the South and a middle way. We had discounted the southerly route as it goes through the edge of the Gobi desert and at this time of year would be very hot. Beside we had already seen plenty of desert landscapes. With the northerly route blocked we set off to ride right through the middle of this huge country.

Mongolia is a landlocked country in east-central Asia. It is bordered by Russia to the north and China to the south, east and west. Ulaanbaatar, the capital and also the largest city, is home to about forty five percent of the population. The area of what is now Mongolia has been ruled by various nomadic empires, including the Xiongnu, the Xianbei, the Rouran, the Turkic Khaganate, and others. In 1206, Genghis Khan founded the Mongol Empire, and his grandson Kublai Khan conquered China to establish the Yuan Dynasty. After the collapse of the Yuan, the Mongols retreated to Mongolia and resumed their earlier pattern of factional conflict and occasional raids on the Chinese borderlands. In the 16th and 17th centuries, Mongolia came under the influence of Tibetan Buddhism. At the end of the 17th century, all of Mongolia had been incorporated into the area ruled by the Manchu's Qing Dynasty. During the collapse of the Qing Dynasty the Mongols established the Temporary Government of Khalkha in November 1911. On 29 December 1911 Mongolia declared independence from the Qing Dynasty and this National Liberation Revolution ended the Manchu's rule that lasted 220 years. The country came under Soviet influence, resulting in the proclamation of the Mongolian People's Republic as a Soviet satellite state in 1924. After the breakdown of communist regimes in Europe in late 1989, Mongolia saw its own democratic revolution in early 1990; it led to a multi-party system, a new constitution in 1992, and transition to a market economy.

At 1,564,116 square kilometres, Mongolia is the 19th largest and the most sparsely populated independent country in the world, with a population of around 2.9 million people. It is also the world's second-largest landlocked country after Kazakhstan. The country contains very little arable land, as much of its area is covered by steppe, with mountains to the north and west and the Gobi Desert to the south. Approximately 30% of the population are nomadic or semi-nomadic. The predominant religion in Mongolia is Tibetan Buddhism. Islam is the dominant religion among ethnic Kazakhs. The majority of the state's citizens are of Mongol ethnicity, although Kazakhs, Tuvans, and other minorities also live in the country, especially in the west. About 20% of the population live on less than about a pound per day. Mongolia joined the World Trade Organization in 1997 and seeks to expand its participation in regional economic and trade regimes. According to a 2011 World Health Organization survey, Mongolia has some of the worst air pollution in the world, but the huge open spaces give no clue that this might be the case.[xxxi]

We were definitely more of a novelty here than in Russia. When we had stopped at the side of the road for lunch there had been nobody in sight. But then three young men arrived as it from nowhere to stand and stare while we ate. People suddenly popping up in a remote place where you thought you were alone was to happen all through Mongolia. The first town we came to was better stocked up than any we had seen in Russia for ages, immediately disproving the idea that all of Mongolia would be a wilderness devoid of the touch of man. Al seemed to be labouring under that misapprehension, but I had a suspicion all along that people wouldn't have found a reason to settle in such massive tracts of land. There was even some mobile phone network cover in places. The roads were badly corrugated gravel which threatened to shatter the hard working suspension of our bikes. Riding alongside the other bike, stood up on the foot pegs at maybe thirty miles an hour, you could see just how hard the forks and swinging arm of each bike was working. They were pounding up and down at a rate that made them appear as a blur. To the rider the bumps felt less severe the faster you dared to go, as instead of hitting each one the bike would seem to skip over the ridges and avoid the dips. These roads continued uninterrupted for miles apart from on the way into one particular town where out of the blue began a single section of pristine, freshly laid black tarmac. It seemed harder to pick out a camp site in this vast and very open countryside. As the light started to fade we speared right away from the road and towards a lake. We chose a spot to camp overlooking the lake and slightly sheltered by the hillside. On the last off road section the rocky ground finally dislodged my bike's exhaust again. The sound of the big single cylinder firing straight out through the cooling fins seemed absolutely deafening in this silent landscape. I almost felt embarrassed for disturbing the peace, even though there was nobody around. I spent the evening trying to reattach the exhaust to the broken studs as best I could.

First thing in the morning we changed Al's tyres back into off road mode and set off around eleven o'clock. We stopped for lunch about one o'clock and had been climbing the whole time. The bike broke down shortly after lunch. Once again it was not breathing properly and Al did not try to hide his displeasure. I changed the spark plug, which was always getting oiled up, and the "air filters". Having also cleaned out the carburettor the bike worked for the rest of the day. In the afternoon we overtook some Swiss and German over-landers travelling by truck. Their achievement and ours in getting this far was put firmly in the shade however, by a German cyclist we met coming the other way. It seemed crazy to me what he was attempting. The road was so rough it was all he could do to turn the pedals. Even for us it was slow progress so far. The tracks we were following were pretty rough and there were a couple of water crossings to negotiate. It was an amazing experience, moving through these huge open vistas and seeing lots of wildlife including herds of camels wandering freely.

We found a nice camp spot next to a stream. When opening one of the cow-photo labelled cans we had bought just before the Russian border we discovered what the shop owner had been trying to warn us of. It was a cow product, but not meat, it was solid yellow cow fat. This lightened the mood somewhat and we developed the concept of throwing rocks at a target one step further. The other unopened and useless can of fat was the target. After several near misses I eventually scored a direct hit on the can with a heavy rock and it burst open squirting the ground with the greasy contents. This passed for great evening entertainment in such a remote location! In the evening it began to rain, so after putting together an alternative dinner of sausage pasta washed down with a little vodka, I crawled into my tent early. We had lost height over the course of the day so it wasn't as cold as the previous night. Despite that, it seemed a long way still to the goal of Ulaanbaatar.

The next morning we reached the town of Kofke, where we bought food and petrol. On the way we met three lads from Oxford delivering a 4X4 ambulance to Ulaanbaatar. We had decided on a different route from them to join back up with the northern trail. We headed back north towards Ulan Gom. There was about twenty five miles of tarmac then the road became very bad. We came across two locals on 150cc scooters who had run out of petrol. We gave them enough to get to the next town and they insisted on paying us. Leading along a straight stretch of gravel road, Al crashed. In places the gravel was deeper and would move under the weight of the bikes and this seemed to have caused the accident. Before I had even managed to fully stop and climb off my bike to help he was up and clearly unhurt. He even gave a pose of bravado for a photo next to the horizontal bike. On picking his bike up though his mood changed dramatically again. The crash had broken his pannier from its mounting. This was the cue for cursing and shouting at me. *Him* crashing *his* bike was my fault somehow! We got the pannier reconnected to the bike using some wire I had brought. Later on that day I crashed myself. The trail had become deep sand, always difficult even for very experienced riders. Crazily the lack of time and energy to change my tyres after the long tarmac sections meant I was still riding on full road tyres. This gave me no grip at all in these conditions. The usual search for a wild camp spot began and we rode off the side of the road and camped in the lee of a rocky peak. We climbed to the top of the outcrop to take in the amazing view. From there we were spotted by two cow herders. They brought their horses up the steep rocky hillside and we took the opportunity for photograph. Communicating only with smiles and gestures we took out new acquaintances down to our camp and shared with them some vodka, Pepsi and chocolates we had with us. We took loads of photographs as they demonstrated their lasso skills on one of their herd. We got to ride their horse around which was great.

The Mongolian horses were small and very placid in character. These young cow hands obviously took good care of their horses as they seemed to be their pride and joy. After a while our new found friends waved goodbye and left, trotting off into the twilight. We carried on with our usual routine but later heard the thumping of horse's hooves on the soft ground coming towards our camp. They had come back in the dark with their own feast to share with us. They brought homemade cheese and curds as well as powerful moonshine. The stars were out and were very bright with so little light pollution around. I continued to nod, smile and think up new ways to try and communicate while sampling the traditional foods. When I was so tired that I could stay awake no longer I waved and headed into my tent. This had been an amazing highlight. I was very grateful that the inquisitive, friendly and generous behaviour of these people had created a total one off experience that I will never forget.

Next morning I landed back in reality with a bump. It was a bad start to the day when Al discovered he'd lost his tool kit yesterday, probably leaving them at the roadside where he had crashed and got the tools out to effect a repair. He set off to look for them on his bike but without the panniers to make it lighter and easier to handle. I intended to spend the time changing my tyres. I was just about to go for a subtle bathroom visit when a goat herder rounded the hill with his flock. I quickly roped him into helping with the bike instead. I got him to hold the back of the bike down so I could change the front tyre. He was very excited to help and really got well into it. We shared some coffee and cake I had to celebrate. After he left I managed to change the back tyre despite the large socket required to remove the axle being one of the things Al was out hunting for. Thankfully I had an adjustable spanner which was just large enough. This was my first ever solo tyre change and it was on uneven ground, on a hill, in deepest Mongolia. Al returned without having been able to locate the missing tools. We made sausage sandwiches for lunch before setting off. We only rode for about four hours making very slow progress over the terrain. Still it was staggering country to be making slow progress in, the views were huge. The ground ranged through grassy to rocky to sandy. We decided to camp early because Al was complaining of back pain and I wasn't going to argue, especially in light of the foul mood he was still in after the loss of the tools. I had a minor problem riding myself as my left hand had been left very swollen from a mosquito bite. I anticipated that we should in any case reach Ulaangom and beyond tomorrow. This was good because I needed cash, petrol and water. By this stage I was also dirty, smelly and hairy! No surprise with the self-sufficient life in the wild I was experiencing.

Day sixty seven of the journey was the twenty eighth of July, Helen's 27th birthday. This must have brought me luck because I found to my shock that Al was in a good mood. This might have been brought on by the improvement in terrain. The land had flattened out and was short grass. There was no track to speak of and it looked as though you could literally ride in any direction you wanted for miles over the virgin ground. The only sign of man was telephone poles carrying wires to some distant town. Even these were far from mundane. Almost every single pole had one or two huge birds of prey perched on top. With the sound of the approaching motorbikes they would spread their wings and gracefully dive from their lofty vantage point. This was the first real full day of riding in Mongolia. We arrived at Ulaangom and after changing money topped up with fuel. Ulaangom is the capital of Uvs Province in Mongolia. It is located 26 km South-West from the lake Uvs Nuur shore and on the slopes of the Kharkhiraa mountain, 120 km south from the Russian border.[xxxii] We bought more food and drink then carried straight on out of the other side. We blasted along off road across the plains for hours. The fun was only punctuated by Al crashing again, and I had a dropped my bike again when I managed to stall and lose my balance. At the end of the day we camped up in the middle of the plain without much shelter. We were probably visible for miles around, but keeping a low profile wasn't required here and nobody bothered us. I almost managed to have the end of planned trip conversation, gently hinting that Mongolia would be the end of this leg for me. The bike was running well despite everything. I had hit a few big ravines today, but nothing had broken and I'd stayed on. Looking out for rocks and these sudden breaks in the surface certainly kept my attention while travelling at over fifty miles an hour off road. Unusually we had a good laugh around dinner. The wine and vodka certainly helped in this regard. We ate a lot of pasta but I never really got bored with it. Today was a nice sausage and tomato pasta dinner. I was also still nibbling on the hard cheese given to us by the friendly cow hands. Even though we'd now been in the country several days I was still amazed by the scale of this place. Sadly it was tinged with the knowledge that I had to continue thinking about my 'exit strategy'. A conversation with Helen was great in this regard and to remind me that there were people around the other side of the world that loved me very much.

Our luck with navigation took a downturn after passing through the next town. Trying to follow Al's GPS we took the wrong route onwards. Each route looked as unlikely as the other. Our choice was bolstered by meeting with some other local bikers who nodded their approval of our route and led us further in that direction. The route was amazing, like being in the Lake District or Yorkshire Dales for miles, but with goats and camels and horses freely trotting around as they pleased. Stopping for lunch we came across a father and two sons who also stopped and passed the time by engaging in their national sport. Mongolian wresting looked tough, and although they were just competing amongst themselves for laughs, there must have been some bruises. Thankfully they didn't ask me to take part, but I did get another ride on one of their horses. As we rode deeper along our chosen route I realised we had gone wrong. Although by now a well-made gravel road, it would stop abruptly at a town built at the end of a valley and surrounded by hills on three sides. The route had no exit on the map other than the way we came. Al began to panic about having to turn around and spend another day going back to where we made the wrong turn. By the time we caught up with where we should have been we would be a couple of days behind schedule. I favoured the idea of trying to forge our own route completely off-piste through the hills. To me the hills looked rolling so we were unlikely to come up against a sheer cliff to bar our way. The ground was still smooth and grassy like most of Mongolia without trees to block our path. If we could only make it over the top of the hills to our left, we would surely be able to drop down into the next valley and would be bound to cross the right route. Al didn't think this idea would work and grumpily said if I wanted to try it I should lead the way. I loved the challenge and set off up the hill, stopping at the last Ger I could see to point in the direction I wanted to go to see their reaction. Although far from conclusive it seemed generally positive, and that was enough. I continued on with adrenaline pumping, my face bursting into a wide grin as I reached a natural pass through the peaks threaded my way through the rockier parts with increasing confidence. The neighbouring valley began to reveal itself. Following nothing more than goat tracks and intuition I was having great fun! With my full off road tyres biting into the soft ground the bike felt composed, so I didn't hold back and sped down the hillside. Periodically I had to sit down on the bike and slow to walking pace to let Al catch up. He shouted at me that I was going far too fast. However I was taking no risks and enjoying it, so I interpreted this as his ego not allowing him to believe that he could not keep up. Al always thought he was the better rider, and he might well have been right, but not there and then. The track through the hills carried us all the way with no problem. As soon as Gers started appearing on this side of the peak it was obvious that they must get their supplies from somewhere, and therefore there must be a way out to civilization in the direction we needed. Persistence and an off road capable bike had won the day. I slowed down and tried to take in my surroundings, there were loads of birds of prey. I'd only ever seen one or two at a time before. They were diving down to grab their prey, which seemed plentiful. Their favourite snack looked like a wee squirrel thing that lived in burrows, where they would try and retreat when danger threatened. Pulling off the road at a quiet spot we made camp. I was satisfied that we'd made it despite everything, including lots of dodgy directions from the locals. It was becoming clear that most didn't understand the concept of a map or how to use one. Beefy stew and vodka ended the day's excitement.

It was a rough night as my sleeping mattress kept deflating. Eventually I found a small cut in it that would mean my nights from now on were much less comfortable. It was the start of another long day. We joined a road which didn't exist on the map but led us to the small town of Altubulab, where we waited ages for petrol. I gave away the last of the sweets I was carrying to the local kids and eventually someone roused the keeper of the petrol pump key. Later we got to an unmarked town near a place called Altay and picked up the main track. We followed it the rest of the day and the time went over very fast. Al shouted at me for getting too far ahead on the track. We were in plain sight of each other, no more than a hundred yards apart in a landscape where you could probably see for five miles. For this reason I decided his ego had landed again and he was upset because he couldn't keep up. We stopped on the way to help a couple of local bikers in trouble. One had a puncture and one a problem with a wheel bearing. We got water and petrol again in Khalban before finding a place to set up camp. There was a spectacular view and it sucked not to be getting the full joy of this place. It is amazing. Navigation is very tricky here and even with a GPS my compass came in very handy! We'd now covered ten thousand eight hundred miles and I was hoping for more good progress the next day.

My prayers were answered and other than a slight problem early on where my luggage came loose and wedged the rear wheel, we continued unhindered. I thankfully found the large bottle oil which fell off in this incident. Al got a puncture on the way into town, the first and only puncture of the whole journey which wasn't self-inflicted during a tyre change. Fixing it at the roadside took one and a quarter hours. Al stubbornly stuck to his ways and still wouldn't change tyres the easy way, using technique rather than brute force. We were about to enter a town called Moron. You can imagine the jokes I was thinking of and insert your own here! We wasted more time looking for a new inner tube in Moron before making a worthwhile visit to a supermarket and petrol station. There seemed to be an in-joke in this town, each of the petrol stations (for some reason this small place had more than one) was clearly unable to lay their hands on 95 octane unleaded petrol. However their signs displaying prices had room for a 95 octane price at the top above the other octanes which were available. Instead of a price the sign read simply 'LOVE'. We thought that we had spotted the correct road out of town forking off from the way we came in. Thankfully I asked anyway at the petrol station to make sure and discovered our assumption was wrong. That saved time and the next five miles out of town towards Ulaanbaatar were tarmac. When the road once more dwindled to nothing, we made camp up on top of a hill. It was unusual because there were some copses of trees. Between them the soft ground was covered in tiny blue flowers. The wind dropped and the view was fantastic. We had a boil-in-bag beef stew for dinner, which must have been the last of the rations I had saved for an emergency. Al dropped some of the piping hot stew in his crotch and I have to admit I found this one of the funniest things ever and was stifling a giggle! All the motorcycle travel and wild camping seemed easy by this stage really, and I was now confident of making it to Ulaanbaatar.

The road from this point on was properly main, in Mongolian terms at least, which translates as many lanes of tyre tracks worn into the dirt! When one path became too rutted the next vehicle through would simply plot a new course alongside the old one. They weren't much fun to ride though. They were faster but also unpredictable as they could quickly change between rocky, sandy, bumpy and dusty. It was not very eventful other than Al's rear tyre puncture repair failing, then failing again, finally re-inflating only to fail again. Putting my 18" rear tube into his 17" rear wheel and tyre solved it, but we weren't sure for how long. Eventually we found a camp spot up the side of a valley in a nature Reserve. The verge of the gravel road was very soft and sandy and in trying to turn off up the hill I was lazy and failed to get my front wheel squared up enough. I dropped the bike, but was so angry with myself for making a stupid mistake at this late point in the day just because I was tired. The anger fuelled my muscles and I heaved the bike upright despite the soft ground without going through any of the usual process of removing luggage to make the load lighter and the task easier. This was probably a bad idea as hurting my back out here could have been a real problem, but I got away with it. Tonight the spaghetti and tuna was accompanied by the now customary wine and shot of vodka. On the map it looked like we would reach the last big town before Ulaanbaatar the next day. I had still not made an absolute decision on an end point for this part of my journey. Al was very hard to talk to about it, getting defensive and angry when he sensed what I might be about to discuss. Part of me really wanted to go on to Vladivostok, on the far side of Russia. However my main concern was which country it would be easier to leave the bike in and depart without a customs issue. My instincts having experienced the two countries and their border officials was that Mongolia would be easier. I knew that as a consequence of westerners dumping their cars when they broke down during the increasingly popular Mongol Rally, the Mongolian government had tightened the rules, but I still felt it was a better bet. There was no mobile signal that day, so I couldn't share my thoughts with anyone and I went to sleep that night feeling very alone.

Ulaanbaatar

I didn't know it at the time, but the camp on the valley side was to be the last. I was expecting another night or maybe even two before reaching Ulaanbaatar, but had reckoned without a huge day of riding. We carried on off road all morning and started following alongside the construction of a new road, which was being built on a scale like nothing we had seen in Mongolia. We couldn't ride on this future dual carriageway yet, but as new roads are built they will certainly change the character of Mongolia forever. The challenge to cross the country will be hugely diminished. We came to the start of the usable tarmac and then into another town. This was the last before Ulaanbaatar. We had planned to go the most direct route from there, but changed our minds when we saw that a route which headed north and joined up with a major road into Ulaanbaatar from the Russian border in the north was tarmac. We couldn't be sure it would go all the way, but we found it did, so we made fast progress. Setting off down this smooth black ribbon the main hazard was a driver who was clearly very drunk and all over the road. The bike started playing up a bit, coughing and spluttering. I suspected more muck in the carburettor, but it pulled through and we made it to the guarded checkpoint entry to Ulaanbaatar!

Ulaanbaatar, literally "Red Hero" is the capital and the largest city of Mongolia. An independent municipality, the city is not part of any province, and its population as of 2008 is over one million. Located in north central Mongolia, the city lies at an elevation of about 1,310 metres in a valley on the Tuul River. It is the cultural, industrial, and financial heart of the country. It is the centre of Mongolia's road network, and is connected by rail to both the Trans-Siberian Railway in Russia and the Chinese railway system. The city was founded in 1639 as a movable Buddhist monastic centre. In 1778, it settled permanently at its present location, the junction of the Tuul and Selbe rivers. Before that, it changed location twenty-eight times, with each location being chosen ceremonially. In the twentieth century, Ulaanbaatar grew into a major manufacturing centre.[xxxiii]

Having looked at a few hotels we checked into one and went out for some dinner. The food was good, but this wasn't quite the full celebration it might have been. I was coming to the conclusion that this was the end of the road, and that a change of plan to something new was needed. The bike and I were both very tired. I would recover physically, but mentally I'd had enough of dealing with a friendship seemingly in tatters. The final straw came when in the middle of the night, while I was soundly sleeping, Al moved out of the double room we had checked into and switched to another room on his own. It was another random decision, as I'd come to expect, which gave no thought to the consequences for me. In this case that I was stuck with the whole bill for the three nights in a large room we had booked in this relatively expensive hotel. Waking up to this news crystallised a plan which had been gradually forming in my mind. Somehow I would fly out of Ulaanbaatar as a normal passenger leaving the bike behind, to Beijing where I could stay with my cousin. This would allow me to see another whole country which wasn't on the original plan, so I was actually pretty excited about it! There were some problems to overcome, particularly working out what to do with the bike to stay legal and how to get a visa to enter China.

I found Al having breakfast and told him my intentions, which he seemed fine with at the time. I spent precious time gifting him all the tools and spares I had to help him continue his journey, while I should have been at the Chinese embassy. Nevertheless I got there just in time to get a visa application form. I ran errands, hitting the internet café and getting more cash at the bank. When I finally went back to hotel I found Al sitting on the wall outside, head down. I walked across the road and up to where he sat and asked if he was OK. He burst into tears. He seemed suddenly convinced he couldn't go on with bike alone. I tried to convince him that he would be fine. It was a very odd situation. He had made me feel like nothing but an inconvenience and a burden on his progress for the last couple of months, yet now I had taken control for myself I was suddenly indispensable. Later on Al came knocking on the door of my room with bottles of beer in hand. He tried to guilt trip me into carrying on and persuaded me to go out for dinner. This was no problem; as far as I was concerned I was perfectly happy to remain friends with no hard feelings! What I wasn't prepared to do was to be mentally abused any longer. We went for beer and pizza and the guilt trip continued. It was all too little too late. I had told Helen and my parents that I was all done, and if he didn't like it well that was tough luck!

I sent Al a message that I wouldn't be able to join him for breakfast as I had to get to the Chinese embassy nice and early to beat the queues. However my plan was foiled when I got there to find it closed. I wasn't the only one. Lola was from Germany and was also suddenly in need of a Chinese visa. Sharing our disappointment at the closed embassy we went for coffee. I must have mentioned the recent story and the price of my hotel. She told me of the hotel she was staying at which was much less expensive and after we'd finished took me there. I was lucky to grab a rare spare bed at the Golden Gobi. While there I met Edward, a very friendly but completely bonkers Irish bloke. Now that I wouldn't be travelling by bike I needed a rucksack for all my gear. I was told of a black market where anything and everything was for sale. I went to where I was told I could find it but having walked for miles, there was nothing there. I set about the other organisational things I needed to do to implement my new plan: got on the internet, changed some cash into dollars and got a fake itinerary from Airmarket. To get a visa for China you needed to have an itinerary showing that your onward travel was booked, but I didn't have any booked, nor did I want to arrange any until I had the visa sorted. I also found a computer specialist and bought an external hard drive large enough to take a copy of the photographs of the trip Al had taken with his camera and had stored away. This was all I had asked for in return for giving him all my spares and tools for free, and he agreed. Somehow I think I knew in my heart that if I didn't get these photographs before we both left Ulaanbaatar, I wouldn't get another opportunity. It was important to have these photographs as well as the ones I had taken as I was on many of them, as he was on mine. I really wanted these memories. Eventually I walked back to the hotel for a rest. Knocked on Al's door to copy the photos, although I could clearly hear the television on in the room he would not answer the door no matter how loudly I knocked.

I still hadn't worked out the legalities of leaving my bike in Mongolia. This is where Helen came to the rescue from thousands of miles away. I'd been relaying my plans to her by email over the last day or so; all the while, without my knowledge, she'd been diligently on travel forums trying to find someone in Ulaanbaatar who could help. Those years of working as a PA for demanding doctors and surgeons had clearly paid off and she found an answer. Miraculously, "Travel buddies" were based in an office just a stone's throw from the Golden Gobi hostel and I went to see them immediately. The girl in the office spoke reassuringly good English and, jovially told me she'd been chatting with Helen back in England and said they could get my bike imported legally, giving me the right paperwork. They would then sell the bike and split the profit with me. Still cautious at this stage, rather than give out my bank details, I said if they could sort everything out then they could keep all the profit. I didn't think they would get much anyway given its condition, and wanted to motivate them that this was a top priority! In the evening, after a visit to the internet café to use their computer to transfer USA maps on to my GPS in readiness for meeting Helen, I was caught in an amazing downpour. To shelter from the rain I dived into a random bar. A large group of young men and women were drinking and chatting in English. I introduced myself and was invited to take a seat. Anyone who knows me will realise that this is extremely out of character for me. Never in a million years would I normally approach a group of strangers and introduce myself so brazenly. I'm a shy Englishman after all. But with the way Al had treated me and buoyed by the self-satisfaction of finally standing up for myself and taking control, I was in the party mood. They turned out to be Israelis and I drank a few beers with them until the rain passed. It had been a hell of a day. It was very uplifting to find help with the bike, especially so randomly, and from the other side of the world, I was now hopeful that this ad hoc plan would all work out in the end.

The next morning I went back to the Chinese Embassy and had entered my Visa application by ten am. I returned and checked out of the hotel, riding to leave my luggage at the Golden Gobi (where I would stay from now on) and carry on to Travel Buddies. So began a bewildering tour of Mongolian bureaucracy. Six of the staff and family who run Travel Buddies, including one young child, piled into a car in a 'how-many-mongolians-can-you-fit-in-a-mini type scenario and I followed them to a test centre. The bike had to have a sort of MOT to ensure its condition was good enough to be eligible for import. Naturally I'm pretty worried about this given the problems I know the bike has. It was subtle, and conducted in Mongolian, but I'm pretty sure that some money changed hands. I cannot imagine how else the bike was able to pass its emissions test, despite the louds of blue oil smoke coming from the exhaust, and pass the lights test despite three of the four indicators clearly not working as they were tested! We had to wait around until two pm for the completed test paperwork as they had gone for their lunch. Next stop was the main police station. Forms were filled in and then we went on to the local district police station. There was a lot of negotiation I couldn't understand. Another journey through town followed, to have some contracts stamped by a notary. This went on so long the English speaking girl took me to a local café and bought me dinner. Finally they seemed happy that everything was in place. I followed the car out of the centre and into the shanty town that stretches up the hillside sprawling away from Ulaanbaatar. The last I see of the bike is when I push it into a lockup shed. Even then it won't go quietly as the door is too narrow; I have to remove one pannier to get it through the gap. It's a sad farewell. Including me, nine people are squeezed into the car in a how-many-mongolians-plus-an-englishman-can-you-fit-in-a-mini, type scenario on the way back to town. It is a Toyota Prius, not the roomiest of cars at the best of times! I remember thinking that it was pretty brave to have such a complicated and relatively expensive car in a country where most people are more familiar with horses. Actually it looked like the driver was more familiar with horses too. I silently nominated him for an imaginary 'World's Worst Driver' award as we careered along. All in all the import process took seven hours. I was to pick up a police letter and certificate the following day. The guys and girls from Travel Buddies worked hard all day and were great. I really hoped that it would work and I could leave without a hitch.

I was up early and went to the French café. Suitably fortified I walked to an outdoor pursuits shop I had spotted, but they didn't open until ten am so I went down the street to a Korean hair salon. I still hadn't had a hair-cut on the whole trip and was something of a mess. Without any shared language it was impossible to get across any details of the cut, not really knowing the Mongolian for 'a short back & sides', so I just surrendered myself to whatever they saw fit to deal out. First they gave me shampoo and head massage, then a hair-cut, then another shampoo, then a hand massage and then a final hair styling. All of this was less than five pounds and I thought my new hair looked very good! I wandered back to the outdoor equipment shop, but found that it was very expensive. Having established that the black market would actually be there today, I headed back in that direction and eventually found a large rucksack for around twenty pounds. On getting back I popped into Travel Buddies to try and get the papers to show I had legitimately disposed of my bike, but they were not ready. I'd also been carrying around a wedge of Kazakh notes since we had arrived at the Kazakhstan border much sooner than expected and not been able to spend them. I took them to lots of different banks, each one suggesting that the next might hold that currency, but I had no joy. I never did manage to change that money into a transferable currency! I had more success with booking my plane ticket to Beijing. With that sorted I went out with Lola and Ed for their last night before they continued with their respective travels. I mentioned Ed was bonkers, and his plan was to go and buy some horses to go travelling through the Mongolian countryside for several weeks. We went to a pizza place and had a very good night out. I talked a lot but they didn't seem to mind! I got back to the hostel to find two snoring Spanish men in the dormitory. This meant not much sleep for me.

In the morning I gave Ed my pans as I didn't really have room to carry them anymore and he could make use of them. Lola, Ed and I all trooped down to the Chinese embassy and were triumphant when we discovered we had all been granted our visas! We went for a celebratory cake and coffee at a little German café. The papers for the bike were still not ready. I spent my lunch catching up with my diary at the Amsterdam café. By now I think I had frequented about every flavour of international café available in Ulaanbaatar and switched to the outdoor café next to the state department store. In the end I got a photocopy of the new Mongolian registration document for the bike, and that was all the paperwork. It wasn't altogether convincing, but they said that when my passport was read the computer system would no longer flag me up as having arrived with a vehicle. I realised I had no choice but to just go for it. They also gave me a present, which was a nice touch! That evening I relaxed hanging out at the hostel, drinking vodka and orange and chatting to a Japanese guy in the dormitory. I also went in search of a bookshop and bought a Lonely Planet city guide to Beijing so that I could read up on things to do and see in China. Late in the evening Mad Ed arrived back at the hostel after the horse deal went sour. He would have to try again another day!

With my flight booked for the following day I wanted to be making the most of my remaining time in Ulaanbaatar by sightseeing, but the torrential rain had started again. I booked a taxi for 2pm the next day, plenty of time before my flight. At the hostel I was asked if I would teach an English lesson, but felt I had to turn them down as I wanted to be free to see the sights if the weather improved. It did, so I went to see a nearby temple. It was good to see some culture even if it wasn't the most impressive example. Walking through the city's central square two guys tried a ruse to pick my pocket by one trying to bump into me and cause a distraction, while the other moved in from behind. I was too quick for them though and got away, letting them know that I knew what they were up to! Later on I spent a bit of time using my IT skills to fix problems with other backpackers' laptops. Another Irish guy bought me a beer for getting the wireless connection to work on his. I also met Claire, who was on her way back to the UK from two years teaching in Japan. For dinner I went back to the Italian restaurant with her and Ed. I very much hoped that this was the last night I would spend in Ulaanbaatar.

China

I waited around impatiently all day for the time to come for my flight. Anxious that there would be no customs problem I went to Genghis Khan Airport really early, but it was pointless since I couldn't start doing anything until check-in opened up. My bag was four kilos overweight but I was let off no problem by the kindly check-in staff. Nobody batted an eyelid at me all through security, and I began to relax thinking that all must be well. Then, out of the blue a uniformed customs official tapped me on the shoulder in the departure lounge and told me to follow him for a "customs check". My heart sank. I followed the official out of the departure lounge and down some stairs. He pushed open some double doors and there was a conveyor belt with some baggage on it. "Yours?" he gestured. I shook my head, these weren't my bags. He grabbed a label on one of the bags and pointed at the name. It read 'David Adams'. I pointed to the surname and shook my head, it wasn't me they were after, it was a case of mistaken identity and my panic was over, I did spare a thought for poor David Adams though, and hope he made it out unscathed, unless of course he was a drug smuggler, in which case I hope he got his comeuppance! The plane was one hour late and on arrival the entry to China was effortless. I got money from a cash machine and took a taxi straight to Gemma's address. The taxi driver was driving like the Top Gear Stig's Chinese cousin, using the hard shoulder to undertake at speed. Gemma's place is a very comfortable apartment in a luxury high rise block. I met baby Henry who was very sleepy and very cute. It was a fantastic decision to come here, I was so excited. This had a real holiday feel and I could just relax at last.

The next few days were a blur, getting used to the sights and sounds of China. Beijing, sometimes known as Peking, is the capital of the People's Republic of China and one of the most populous cities in the world. The population as of 2013 was 21,150,000. The metropolis, located in northern China, is governed as a direct-controlled municipality under the national government, with 14 urban and suburban districts and two rural counties. Beijing Municipality is surrounded by Hebei Province with the exception of neighbouring Tianjin Municipality to the southeast.

Beijing is the second largest Chinese city by urban population after Shanghai and is the nation's political, cultural, and educational centre. It is home to the headquarters of most of China's largest state-owned companies, and is a major hub for the national highway, expressway, railway, and high-speed rail networks. The Beijing Capital International Airport is the second busiest in the world by passenger traffic. All of this was something of a shock after the small towns and isolation of the last few months. The city's history dates back three millennia. As the last of the Four Great Ancient Capitals of China, Beijing has been the political centre of the country for much of the past eight centuries. The city is renowned for its opulent palaces, temples, parks and gardens, tombs, walls and gates, and its art treasures and universities have made it a centre of culture and art in China. Encyclopaedia Britannica notes that "few cities in the world have served for so long as the political headquarters and cultural centre of an area as immense as China".[xxxiv]

After catching up with Gemma, I walked down to the local police station to register with them, a requirement when not staying in a hotel. I was surprised at the local supermarket to see that they had tanks of live fish from which you could choose which to buy to take home and cook for dinner. I went out for dinner with Gemma, her husband Allan and her friend Jessica. First on my list of must see sights, being the rebel that I am, was the Forbidden City. The Forbidden City was the Chinese imperial palace from the Ming dynasty to the end of the Qing dynasty. It is located in the centre of Beijing, China, and now houses the Palace Museum. For almost 500 years, it served as the home of emperors and their households, as well as the ceremonial and political centre of Chinese government.

Built in 1406 to 1420, the complex consists of 980 buildings and covers 180 acres. The palace complex exemplifies traditional Chinese palatial architecture, and has influenced cultural and architectural developments in East Asia and elsewhere. The Forbidden City was declared a World Heritage Site in 1987, and is listed by UNESCO as the largest collection of preserved ancient wooden structures in the world. Since 1925, the Forbidden City has been under the charge of the Palace Museum, whose extensive collection of artwork and artefacts were built upon the imperial collections of the Ming and Qing dynasties. Part of the museum's former collection is now located in the National Palace Museum in Taipei. Both museums descend from the same institution, but were split after the Chinese Civil War.[xxxv]

Gemma gave me her underground pass to use which was brilliant, as this allowed me to hop on and off the excellent Beijing underground system as I pleased. I tried to walk around every part of this vast compound and tried to imagine what life would have been like here in its heyday. To get a better idea of the true scale of the place I climbed up the hill through the park behind the city and took in the view. Back at the apartment I had an email from makers of Long Way Round. They had come across my blog and wanted me to write a contribution to a new website they were launching. I wrote something as quickly as I could and sent it back to them with a photo. They published it on the web shortly after, making me feel famous for at least one of my fifteen minutes! Having a computer at my disposal was a luxury and I used it to call home via Skype and to hunt for a flight for the next leg of my journey. The plan had solidified into a couple of weeks in Beijing followed by meeting up with Helen for a couple of weeks in California. Helen was organising the details for that, then I would set off by myself again for a long road trip around America. I needed a suitable vehicle for this new adventure and opted for a Ford Mustang. I thought that this had the required style and American-ness to fit the bill nicely. Dinner was authentic Chinese Dumplings, which set the tone for wonderful food throughout my stay. Camp stove pasta was a thing of the past!

In the following days I took the tube line 10 to the far end then walked to the Summer Palace. The Summer Palace is a vast ensemble of lakes, gardens and palaces in Beijing. It's mainly dominated by Longevity Hill and the Kunming Lake. It covers an expanse of 2.9 square kilometres, three-quarters of which is water.

Longevity Hill is about 60 metres (200 feet) high and has many buildings positioned in sequence. The front hill is rich with splendid halls and pavilions, while the back hill, in sharp contrast, is quiet with natural beauty. The central Kunming Lake covering 2.2 square kilometres was entirely man-made and the excavated soil was used to build Longevity Hill. In the Summer Palace, one finds a variety of palaces, gardens, and other classical-style architectural structures.

In December 1998, UNESCO included the Summer Palace on its World Heritage List. It declared the Summer Palace "a masterpiece of Chinese landscape garden design. The natural landscape of hills and open water is combined with artificial features such as pavilions, halls, palaces, temples and bridges to form a harmonious ensemble of outstanding aesthetic value." It is a popular tourist destination but also serves as a recreational park.[xxxvi] It was a good day out and I liked it better than the Forbidden City. More people wanted their photo taken with a foreigner, and I was happy to oblige! There are fewer and fewer places in the world where having different coloured skin and different features make you a celebrity. I also went to see some of the modern side of the city. New architecture in Beijing can be very controversial as I found out. I went to the "birds nest" Olympic stadium and water cube built for the Beijing Olympics. I mistimed this though as I think they are more spectacular when lit up at night. Most controversial of all is the CCTV building. I was just busy taking some photographs of this towering glass and steel structure when a random Chinese gentleman walked over. Summoning all the English he could muster he told me how terrible he thought it was and how it was shaped like my shorts. I could kind of see his point, but I also was impressed by the architecture and engineering that had gone into creating the massive overhanging "crotch". Having a new baby in the house, Gemma and Allan were understandably busy. But being good hosts wanted me to get out and experience Beijing nightlife as well as the tourist spots. The best way to do this was to head out in the evening with Jessica when she was available. We went for dinner at a US style place after which we hit some bars for shooters and cocktails. I had a great time, and we had lots of fun playing pool until the early hours of the morning.

After such a late finish I still managed to get as far as Riton Park. It was nice, but not on the scale of the major sights. Gemma and Allan took me to their local restaurant where Allan would keep getting the waiters to go into the kitchen and bring back the ingredients that went into the different dishes to show me. This included the still swimming fish!

Looking for presents to eventually take back to the UK, I took the opportunity to shop at the antiques market. I bought some presents after a good haggle. I probably still paid way too much, but never mind, the young lad was good value and happily bantered back and forth using whatever means we could to get the message across. One of the most bizarre moments in Beijing happened when I went for noodles at the nearby Carrefour supermarket. A frustrated shopper, apparently enraged by the heavy traffic, went mad in the car park and rammed his way out in a movie style, damaging numerous cars as he made his escape!

It was time for the big one. I set off to walk the Great Wall of China at Badaling. The Great Wall of China is a series of fortifications made of stone, brick, tamped earth, wood, and other materials, generally built along an east-to-west line across the historical northern borders of China in part to protect the Chinese Empire or its prototypical states against intrusions by various nomadic groups or military incursions by various warlike peoples or forces. Several walls were being built as early as the 7th century BC; these, later joined together and made bigger and stronger, are now collectively referred to as the Great Wall. Especially famous is the wall built between 220–206 BC by the first Emperor of China, Qin Shi Huang. Little of that wall remains. Since then, the Great Wall has on and off been rebuilt, maintained, and enhanced; the majority of the existing wall fragments are from the Ming Dynasty.

Other purposes of the Great Wall have included border controls, allowing the imposition of duties on goods transported along the Silk Road, regulation or encouragement of trade and the control of immigration and emigration. Furthermore, the defensive characteristics of the Great Wall were enhanced by the construction of watch towers, troop barracks, garrison stations, signalling capabilities through the means of smoke or fire, and the fact that the path of the Great Wall also served as a transportation corridor.

The main Great Wall line stretches from Shanhaiguan in the east, to Lop Lake in the west, along an arc that roughly delineates the southern edge of Inner Mongolia. A comprehensive archaeological survey, using advanced technologies, has concluded that the Ming walls measure 5,500 miles. This is made up of 3,889 miles of sections of actual wall, 223 miles of trenches and 1,387 miles of natural defensive barriers such as hills and rivers. Another archaeological survey found that the entire wall with all of its branches measure out to be 13,171 miles.[xxxvii]

I started feeling queasy on the underground, always a dreaded feeling in case it precedes a severe bout of illness. I located the correct bus no problem, but there was a big queue. While waiting I met an older Korean couple and reassured them they were in the right place. It was an odd moment as I had initially taken them for Chinese, so assumed that they could read the signs. I spent nearly three hours at the Wall which was very busy. I walked as far along it as was possible in either direction. Arriving back at the bus stop I had to queue for the bus home for over an hour. This wasn't going down well and there were arguments, pushing and shoving to get on! I made it, but I had to stand up all the way back. In a typical moment of Chinese organisation the driver even had to make a stop for more fuel! I had felt ill on and off all day, but it didn't ruin the experience. The wall is impressive but with all the people and because it had been heavily reconstructed in that area it wasn't as authentic or magical as it might have been. The conditions were also very foggy so the views were limited.

I looked around the Temple of Heaven park but by this stage was getting pretty "templed-out". They all started to look fairly similar, and I was missing the action of being on the move every day. I headed back to Tiananmen Square, which I had seen briefly on my visit to the Forbidden City. Tiananmen Square is a large city square in the centre of Beijing, named after the Tiananmen gate (Gate of Heavenly Peace) located to its North, separating it from the Forbidden City. Tiananmen Square is the fourth largest city square in the world at 440,000 square metres. It has great cultural significance as it was the site of several important events in Chinese history.

Outside China, the square is best known in recent memory as the focal point of the Tiananmen Square protests of 1989, a pro-democracy movement which ended on 4 June 1989 with the declaration of martial law in Beijing by the government and the shooting of several hundred or possibly thousands of civilians by soldiers.[xxxviii] I hoped to see a lot more, but the Chairman Mao Memorial Hall and the Hall of the People were both closed. The Quinmen at the opposite end of the square from the Forbidden City was covered in scaffolding, so it wasn't the best time to be visiting. I wandered off through a "Hutong" area, which is what they call the ancient backstreets, looking for old world magic, but didn't find anything mysterious. The final temple I saw was the Lama Temple. I liked it better than most others; it was a bit different to the rest because of the Buddhist influence. Climbing the ancient sites, the Bell and Drum Towers provided good views and some bite- sized culture. Gulou, the drum tower of Beijing, is situated at the northern end of the central axis of the Inner City to the north of Di'anmen Street. Originally built for musical reasons, it was later used to announce the time and is now a tourist attraction.

Zhonglou, the bell tower of Beijing, stands closely behind the drum tower. Together with the drum tower, they provide an overview of central Beijing and before the modern era, they both dominated Beijing's ancient skyline.[xxxix] Talking of bite sized, I couldn't leave Beijing with trying some Beijing (Peking) Duck, and I took Gemma and Allan to lunch to thank them for their amazing hospitality. With time in China running out, I just had to focus on packing up and planning the next leg, back on the road.

USA

The flights from Beijing to Los Angeles via Taipei went OK, my only worry being if everything would keep to time. If it did I should land at LAX airport within half an hour of Helen arriving on her flight from the UK. US immigration at LAX were their usual selves and it took over an hour to get through. The airport arrivals hall was in the middle of refurbishment and a degree of chaos had ensued. Neither of us was sure we were in the right place, but thankfully after making it through baggage claim I saw her pretty smiling face from across the arrivals hall. Meeting up with Helen was very joyful, we dropped our bags and hugged in the arrivals hall, it was good to have human contact again. I stared at her face for about 2 minutes just checking she was real, much to the annoyance of an American businessman who tutted in disgust! We happily set off to pick up our hire car, but this ended up taking two hours after Helen misread the confirmation and we got the shuttle bus to the Dollar car park instead of Alamo. I was tired and starting to regret the decision to head straight out of LA as the drive to Las Vegas seemed like a long way; not that I said any of this to Helen though. I didn't want her to think I was having a dig after having been so happy to see each other moments earlier. We stopped only to pick up some all American burgers on the way, which were very welcome after all of the aeroplane food. Checking into our room at the Stratosphere Hotel and Casino we could finally have some privacy. Or so we thought, it wasn't long before we were interrupted mid-smooch by the delivery of an entire refrigerator to our room. Handy for keeping some drinks cool. Our room was several stories up and had a large window with a wide ledge. Jet lag induced sleep followed and we were both awake at the crack of dawn so ventured to the nearest Denny's for breakfast. After living off ration packs for the last few months a big greasy breakfast felt like I was dining like a king. We tried to stay out of the hot sun by wandering through the casinos, stopping for coffees here and there. It was weird being with someone again. One particular time we'd had a coffee in Starbucks and when I'd finished I just got up and walked off leaving Helen there on her own! I wasn't used to having to think about another person and check whether she'd finished or not! We bought some booze at the local off licence (may as well use that fridge now we had it!) and sat on the window ledge looking out at the view over the strip, talking and having a few drinks. The tiredness and alcohol combined with the relief of seeing Helen again to shatter the remainder of reserve I had left. As the realisation hit that I had survived and that we were back together, I broke down into tears.

August in Las Vegas is hot. Very hot. As soon as we got out of bed every morning we went out sunbathing straight away at the hotel's pool area. This was luxury beyond what I was used to, with waitresses circulating to bring drinks to your sun lounger. It wasn't long before we were melting; Helen in particular who is very blonde, didn't cope all that well in the spiralling desert heat and had to beat a hasty retreat to the air-conditioned comfort of the hotel. We took a walk around some of the famous Las Vegas strip, taking in the bright lights and noise of the many casinos. We went to a diner for a dinner of salad. However we were still very tired after only about three hours sleep, so bed wasn't long in coming.

The next day we had recovered a bit more and grabbed a few more of the sun's rays before deciding to jump on the monorail to the MGM Grand Hotel at the other end of the strip. We were in party mood and made do with a pretzel for lunch, focussing instead on two "yards of cocktail" each. These yards were plastic versions of the traditional "yard of ale" but weren't actually a yard long. However they could be refilled at various outlets with any of a variety of flavours of frozen Margarita, so we explored the bottom end of the strip giggling happily under their influence. Having seen a lot of Las Vegas already on previous trips, we decided to check out the older parts and look for a little taste of the authentic. We got the latter in the form of a Carne Asada Burrito from a dodgy looking Mexican cafe. The surroundings might have been down to earth, but the Burrito was out of this world, packed full of delicious meat and traditional fillings and the local Mexican contingent of Vegas who were dining there as well made us feel very welcome. Suitably fortified we carried on to Fremont, the older downtown area and original Vegas strip. This place has a bit of old Americana charm, but its glory is somewhat faded and looks like it will struggle to compete with the glitz of the new strip and the mega hotels. The next few days we relaxed and took it easy. A blur of sunbathing and buffets that wasn't probably a good idea! We did "normal" things like check out shops and go to the cinema. The final blowout in Vegas was the Stratosphere's own all-you-can-drink Margaritas and Martinis. We paid around twenty dollars and the drinks are free for four hours. Apparently afterwards we watched "Hitch" on the TV, but I can't remember that at all, or having anything to eat. As far as I am concerned the hours between eight that evening and waking up the next morning will be forever lost! On the plus side though it was probably the best sleep I'd had since arriving in the states! Spurred on to do something a bit more constructive we headed out to Red Rock Canyon.

Red Rock Canyon State Park features scenic desert cliffs (mainly red), buttes (red with yellow) and spectacular rock formations (also red). The park is located where the southernmost tip of the Sierra Nevada Mountains converges with the El Paso Range and each little canyon is unique, with dramatic shapes and vivid colours.

Tourist information reveals that historically, the area was once home to the Kawaiisu Indians, who left petroglyphs in the El Paso Mountains and other evidence of their inhabitation. As a result this place was on the Native American trade route for thousands of years. During the early 1870s, the colourful rock formations in the park served as landmarks for 20-mule team freight wagons that stopped for water. About 1850, it was used by the footsore survivors of the famous Death Valley trek including members of the Arcane and Bennett families along with some of the Illinois Jayhawkers. The park now protects significant palaeontology sites and the remains of 1890s-era mining operations, and has been the site for a number of movies.

After wet winters, the park's floral displays are stunning. The beauty of the desert combined with the geologic features make this park a camper's favourite destination. Apparently wildlife you may encounter includes roadrunners, hawks, lizards, mice and squirrels. I don't remember spotting any of those but there are definitely miles of trails that meander through the dramatic landscape of the park. I did see some locals flying around on off road quad bikes. I assumed that this was probably illegal, as things like that are usually very much frowned upon in the UK. However I later found out that all licensed vehicles may travel on the primitive dirt road system within the park as long as the drivers are licenced also and they don't create new routes of their own. Drinking and driving laws still apply to both on the paved and primitive dirt roads though, so it's not completely a free for all![xl]

On day 101 since leaving home it was time to leave the excesses of Vegas. We drove to 29 Palms, a quaint motel very unlike any of the chain motels found everywhere in the states. This was our accommodation while we had a look around the Joshua Tree National Park. Joshua Tree National Park is immense, nearly 800,000 acres, and infinitely variable. It can seem unwelcoming, even brutal during the heat of summer when, in fact, it is delicate and extremely fragile. This is a land shaped by strong winds, sudden torrents of rain, and climatic extremes. Rainfall is sparse and unpredictable. Streambeds are usually dry and waterholes are few. Viewed in summer, this land may appear defeated and dead, but within this parched environment are intricate living systems waiting for the opportune moment to reproduce. The individuals, both plant and animal, that inhabit the park are not individualists. They depend on their entire ecosystem for survival.

Two deserts, two large ecosystems primarily determined by elevation, come together in the park. Few areas more vividly illustrate the contrast between "high" and "low" desert. Below 3,000 feet (910 m), the Colorado Desert (part of the Sonoran Desert), occupying the eastern half of the park, is dominated by the abundant creosote bush. Adding interest to this arid land are small stands of spidery ocotillo and cholla cactus. The higher, slightly cooler, and wetter Mojave Desert is the special habitat of the undisciplined Joshua tree, extensive stands of which occur throughout the western half of the park. According to legend, Mormon pioneers considered the limbs of the Joshua trees to resemble the upstretched arms of Joshua leading them to the promised land. Others were not as visionary. Early explorer John Fremont described them as "...the most repulsive tree in the vegetable Kingdom."

Standing like islands in a desolate sea, oases provide dramatic contrast to their arid surroundings. Five fan palm oases dot the park, indicating those few areas where water occurs naturally at or near the surface, meeting the special life requirements of those stately trees. Oases once serving earlier desert visitors now abound in wildlife. The park encompasses some of the most interesting geologic displays found in California's deserts. Rugged mountains of twisted rock and exposed granite monoliths testify to the tremendous earth forces that shaped and formed this land. Arroyos, playas, alluvial fans, bajadas, pediments, desert varnish, granites, aplite, and gneiss interact to form a giant mosaic of immense beauty and complexity.

As old as the desert may look, it is but a temporary phenomenon in the incomprehensible time-scale of geology. In more verdant times, one of the Southwest's earliest inhabitants, members of the Pinto Culture, lived in the now dry Pinto Basin. Later, Indians travelled through this area in tune with harvests of pinyon nuts, mesquite beans, acorns, and cactus fruit, leaving behind rock paintings and pottery ollas as reminders of their passing. In the late 1800s cattlemen came to the desert. They built dams to create water tanks. They were followed by miners who tunnelled the earth in search of gold. They are gone now, but they left behind the Lost Horse and Desert Queen mines and the Keys Ranch. In the 1930s homesteaders came seeking free land and the chance to start new lives. Today many people come to the park's 794,000 acres of open space seeking clear skies and clean air, and the peace and tranquillity, the quietude and beauty, only deserts offer.

Desert vegetation, often appearing to have succumbed to this hot sometimes unrelentedly dry environment, lies dormant, awaiting the rainfall and moderate weather that will trigger its growth, painting the park a profusion of colours. At the edges of daylight and under clear night skies live a number of generally unfamiliar desert animals. Waiting out daytime heat, these creatures run, hop, crawl, and burrow in the slow rhythm of desert life. Under bright sun and blue sky, bighorn sheep and golden eagles add an air of unconcerned majesty to this land.

For all its harshness, the desert is a land of extreme fragility. Today's moment of carelessness may leave lasting scars or disrupt an intricate system of life that has existed for eons. When viewed from the roadside, the desert only hints at its hidden life. To the close observer, a tiny flower bud or a lizard's frantic dash reveals a place of beauty and vitality. [xli] It is a fascinating landscape and we took a walk to an interesting dried up dam. It was shocking to see how the environment here has changed so radically in the last hundred years. Clearly at one time the dam would have formed a small reservoir, but now there was nothing but dust. We dined on wine and chicken salad in our private courtyard, staring up at the stars.

Time to move on again and after a late start having done a little sunbathing around the pool, we made the drive to San Diego. For Helen the main attraction of San Diego was the world famous zoo, and we spent all day there. The 100-acre Zoo is home to over 3,700 rare and endangered animals representing more than 650 species and subspecies, and a prominent botanical collection with more than 700,000 exotic plants. It is located just north of downtown San Diego in Balboa Park.[xlii] Under an oppressive blazing sun, the animals were coping a lot better than us! In the evening we found a local Mexican restaurant and feasted on their amazing steak and chicken kebabs and shrimp tacos.

Suitably inspired by the Mexican food, we decided on taking a day trip over the border to Mexico. Tijuana is the nearest town on the Mexico side of the border from San Diego, and getting there was easy enough.

We parked up and crossed the border as pedestrians. Tijuana is renowned for its seedier side, and in terms of things to do without indulging in drugs or prostitution (hotel rooms can be rented by the hour), there isn't much there. As soon as you venture off the main tourist trap there are many scantily clad women hanging around darkened doorways waiting for business to come their way. We had lunch outside under a canopy on the main drag. A local artist drew our caricature, but not it the mood to be ripped off I wasn't going to pay for something we hadn't asked for. Disappointed the man tore off the picture and tossed it onto our table for free anyway. After a walk around we bought tequila and some Cuban cigars before cutting our losses and heading back over the border. It was a sad way to see a glimpse of a country. I felt that judging Mexico on Tijuana would be like coming to the UK but only seeing a Liverpool council estate in the rain before condemning the whole country. In the evening we went to a local comedy night. The "improv" style show was very good. The small, half full theatre belied the quality of the comedians. Other than that our highlight of San Diego nightlife was a visit to the Gaslamp district where we had a couple of beers at the Yard House. They claim to have the most draft beers available anywhere in the world. I don't know if that is true, but they had enough to make only choosing a couple into a major problem! The Gaslamp Quarter is a district of San Diego, California. It is a historical neighbourhood in Downtown San Diego, and is the site of several entertainment and night life venues, as well as scheduled events and festivals. PETCO Park, home of the San Diego Padres is located one block away in downtown San Diego's East Village.

The area is listed as a historic district on the National Register of Historic Places as Gaslamp Quarter Historic District. Its main period of development began in 1867, when Alonzo Horton bought the land in hopes of creating a new city centre closer to the bay, and chose 5th Avenue as its main street. After a period of urban decay, the neighbourhood underwent urban renewal in the 1980s and 1990s. The Gaslamp Quarter extends from Broadway to Harbor Drive, and from 4th to 6th Avenue, covering 16½ blocks. It includes 94 historic buildings, most of which were constructed in the Victorian Era, and are still in use with active tenants including restaurants, shops and nightclubs.[xliii]

The following day we left San Diego and drove to Newport, just a hundred miles away. The hotel there was the same chain as the one in San Diego but much nicer. We tried to go to Balbora Beach, but this tiny peninsula was crammed with the beautiful people of LA and was far too busy to park. We took to sunbathing at our deserted hotel pool instead. Dinner that night was a truly American affair, an endless orgy of shrimp, mostly skewered with all kinds of flavoured glazes. I joined in with the American way and managed to get through nine refills! Our next beach visit was more successful at Corona del mar. Although it was very busy again, I could see why. It's a beautiful area with expensive houses lining the cliff top. Part of me yearned for a deserted version of this beach though! I consoled myself with the thought that I would soon be checking out some of the lesser known corners of the USA.

California

I dropped Helen off at LAX airport for another tearful goodbye. I think this time though she felt more reassured that I was coming home to her and that we would only be apart another month; after the 3 months we'd just endured, this seemed like a walk in the park! I picked up the Mustang as my new transport and headed North, cruising up highway 101. There were great views of the sea at some points. The Mustang's satellite radio seemed to be inspired and played 'Eye of the Tiger' then 'Walking on Sunshine' followed by Van Halen, Def Leppard and AC/DC. I was enjoying the new wheels. The car had electric power controls for everything from windows to seats. Most importantly, each time I got out of it I thought it looked so bloody cool! It wasn't really fast despite the large engine, but much better than the average hire car. When I rolled into my hotel in Lompoc, I was pleased to find it was opposite a supermarket. This was very handy on the first evening back on my own for picking up something to drink and traditional US style fried chicken for dinner. Lompoc is known as the City of Arts and Flowers, and is a small town with a population of about 45,000 located right at the heart of the Central Coast.

Additionally, it is also home to a Federal Penitentiary and located just next to Vandenberg Air Force Base, known for being the only base in the US that launches missiles into polar orbit. Not only that, it has been featured in movies such as Sideways and The Fast and Furious.[xliv] It was odd to be alone, and I felt I would need to re adjust into this new mode of travel. That night I connected to the next door hotel's WIFI for free, instead of the one I was staying in. This amused me greatly as it saved me a whopping $2.99! I researched where I might end up over the next month while easing my nerves with some Keystone Light.

I got up at nine in the morning; but was feeling a bit down, as it was still weird being on my own. Highway one takes a while to get going but is pretty spectacular when it does. It runs right along the California coast, the road followed the coastal inlets, so each rounding of the next corner was an opportunity for a new panorama to unveil itself. This was the first proper test of the Mustang. As it turned out its handling was rubbish on the twisty sections! What did I expect from an American "muscle car"? In tight corners the weight of the car moved around uncomfortably on its suspension and the tyres squealed at anything above walking pace. I visited Big Sur, famous for its surfing and hippie roots, but didn't find much that appealed, so carried on to look around Monterey's fisherman's wharf. Fisherman's Wharf is lined with seafood restaurants ranging from casual, open-air clam bars, to formal indoor dining with views of the bay. Along with Cannery Row, Fisherman's Wharf is one of the few areas in Monterey that sells souvenirs, so the restaurants are interspersed with gift shops, jewellery stores, art galleries, and candy shops. Whale watching tours and fishing trips leave from the wharf, and sea lions often sleep on the pilings, buoys, and moored boats in the bay.

At the entrance to the wharf is Custom House Plaza, the historical centre of Monterey. The Custom House is the first government building in California and the location where the United States took Monterey from Mexico in 1846. The Monterey Maritime Museum is also located in Custom House Plaza, detailing both the maritime and cultural history of Monterey and the surrounding area. Many other historic buildings are located in this plaza. It is also the location of the last whalebone sidewalk in the United States.

Accessible almost exclusively to pedestrians, Fisherman's Wharf is located at the end of the Alvarado Mall, just west of the municipal wharf on Lighthouse Avenue. It is also on the Coastal Recreation Trail, providing pedestrian access to Cannery Row and Pacific Grove from Memorial Day to Labor Day the city of Monterey provides a free trolley service to Cannery Row and the Monterey Bay Aquarium. A favourite activity on the wharf, for both tourists and locals, is sailing on the Monterey Bay along Cannery Row.[xlv] I moved on to Marina to spend the night. They have an ambitious vision that Marina "will grow and mature from a small town bedroom community to a small city which is diversified, vibrant and through positive relationships with regional agencies, self-sufficient. The City will develop in a way that insulates it from the negative impacts of urban sprawl to become a desirable residential and business community in a natural setting." [xlvi] They're going to need some patience with that because this place doesn't have much to it, even their Walmart was lacking in food choices. It was a good job that fuel was still relatively cheap in the US because the Mustang was drinking it at an alarming rate! This is despite the V6 engine which is the American idea of fuel efficient, and I suppose compared to an even bigger V8 they're right! It didn't feel very environmentally friendly, but when in Rome...

After another night's sleep I felt better about travelling alone. It wasn't anything practical which bothered me, I was not concerned about security and when busy during the day perfectly happy with my own company. In fact; doing just as I pleased without anyone else to consider was liberating. Only in the evenings was it a challenge, with nobody to "download" and discuss the day's sights and sounds with, they somehow felt emptier. I booked some more motels for the next few nights in the morning and set off around 11:30. It was an easy cruise stopping at a reservoir on the way and eating Mexican food. I took a detour on the route via Newman, CA as I couldn't pass up the opportunity for a photograph next to various signs with my name on them. I arrived at my hotel for the night shortly after three and relaxed at the pool until five. The weather was suddenly much hotter having driven inland from the coast. I dealt with practicalities like washing clothes and killed time watching films, taking it easy in preparation for an early start and a big day at the Yosemite National Park to come.

National Parks

As I knew it would be a long day, I was up and at Yosemite by 9:30am. Yosemite National Park, which boasts nearly 95 percent designated Wilderness, is a 195-mile escape from urban San Francisco or a 315-mile journey from Los Angeles. The expansive park's 747,956 acres or 1,169 square miles are home to hundreds of wildlife species and thousands of Yosemite plants. Designated a World Heritage Site in 1984, Yosemite is known for its granite cliffs, waterfalls, clear streams, giant sequoia groves and biological diversity. Two Wild & Scenic Rivers, the Tuolumne and Merced rivers, begin in the park and flow west to the Central Valley. Visitors experience the park's 800 miles of hiking trails and 282 miles of road.

Yosemite supports more than 400 species of vertebrates, including fish, amphibians, reptiles, birds, and mammals. Insects abound as well, with the recent discovery of two species not believed to exist anywhere else in the world. The high diversity of animal species falls in line with striking gradient and topographic variability of the park. Move up or down in elevation and you feel as though you are in another park. Vegetation changes from oak woodlands to chaparral scrublands to lower montane to upper montane to subalpine to alpine. In the alpine zone you can see krummholz whitebark pines and perhaps a western juniper or mountain hemlock. Scientists study many individual plants, including the black oak, to understand its future challenges.

Yosemite is a scientific laboratory of hydrology, geology and glaciology, amongst other sciences. Visitors fall in love with the park's many waterfalls, specifically 2,425-foot Yosemite Falls that ranks as the tallest in North America, flowing down into the scenic Valley meadows. Hikers take notice of the enormous granite mountains from the 8,842-foot Half Dome to the 13,114-foot Mt. Lyell-Yosemite's tallest peak.

Glaciers, which John Muir sought out in California as well as Alaska, add into the mix with the Maclure and Lyell still intact. [xlvii] The scenery is wonderful, waterfalls cascading down the side of cliffs as I drove along. I navigated up to Glacier Point, but this took a long time as there were really bad road works. The view from the top made it worthwhile. I had to get out of the car and explore in more detail, so I took a very steep five mile hike to the top of Vernal Fall. This was very tiring in the heat! Vernal Fall is one of the falls in the park which flows all year. At the time I was there the dry summer had taken its toll on those falls that rely on winter rains or spring snow melt to make them run. I drove around the valley back to one of the three giant sequoia groves in the park. Giant sequoias are the world's largest single trees and largest living thing by volume. Giant sequoias grow to an average height of fifty to eighty five metres and six to eight metres in diameter. Record trees have been measured to be nearly ninety five metres in height and over seventeen metres in diameter. The oldest known giant sequoia based on ring count is 3,500 years old. Giant Sequoias are among the oldest living things on Earth.[xlviii] Although not the biggest examples in California there were still some massive trees here.

After walking around the trees and trying in vain to get the scale of them captured on camera, I started out of the park. It was a good twisty road and I was having fun until I crested a rise and saw a Park Ranger with a speed gun sitting in his 4X4. I slowed down but sure enough a few moments later I was being pulled over to the side of the road. The Ranger informed me that I had been doing sixty eight miles an hour in what was a forty five mile an hour zone. This could mean trouble! He asked me for my drivers' licence and to stay in the car. I handed over my licence and waited. The ranger walked back over and to my surprise told me to slow down, before handing back my licence and getting back into his vehicle. He had let me go without any penalty! I could only assume that the foreign licence meant that it was more trouble than it was worth to issue a ticket. I duly stuck to the limits and made it to my motel in Carson City around eight. Carson City looked small to me, just a single main road with hotels and fast food outlets. It certainly didn't seem like a city and perhaps with just fifty five thousand inhabitants that's no surprise. By this time it was dark and I was pretty tired and accidentally went to reception at the hotel next door! The receptionist realised my mistake and pointed me in the right direction. I collapsed into the room and ordered pizza online. The online tracker worked brilliantly and the pizza came right to my door. A miracle of the modern age!

I woke up the next morning with sore legs from the exertion of Yosemite! It was OK though as it was due to be a proper road trip day today. It was a long drive through some great scenery. I set off after talking to Helen and catching the second half of Liverpool – Burnley. I'd been football starved for months, and even though I'm not a fanatic, it was nice to see some English football. If you're interested, Liverpool won four nil. I picked up some cash and fuel in Carson City, and then only stopped for coffee and apple pie on the way. The Mustang's trip computer nearly caused me a major problem. I passed the last petrol station having consulted the remaining miles of fuel compared to the miles left to my destination and noted I should make it easily. However the freeway seemed to be uphill all the way from then on. The miles remaining on the trip computer plummeted. As its neared zero I pulled off the freeway, not wanting to run out on a major road with no hard shoulder. Thankfully the road I turned on to continued parallel and directly towards town. I finally crested the top of the hill and rolled down the other side into Wendover with 0 miles of fuel showing on the trip computer. It was worrying to say the least, and I was very pleased to find the first building on the way into town was a petrol station where I gleefully refilled the tank. At one of my many fuel stops the girl working the till couldn't understand why on earth I would be in her backwater town all the way from England. I got the distinct impression she would have quite happily jumped in the car and set off into the sunset! Wendover is like a mini Las Vegas on the border line of Nevada and Utah, near Salt Lake City. I was already thinking of the reason I was here, and drove out to the Bonneville Salt Flats. Imagine a place so flat you seem to see the curvature of the planet, so barren not even the simplest life forms can exist. Imagine the passing thunder of strange vehicles hurtling by on a vast dazzling white plain. This is not an alien world far from earth; it is Utah's famous Bonneville Salt Flats.

The Bonneville Salt Flats is one of the most unique natural features in Utah. Stretching over 30,000 acres, the Bonneville Salt Flats is a fragile resource administered by the Bureau of Land Management. It is located along I-80 near the Utah-Nevada border. Wendover is the closest city. Thousands of visitors, commercial filmmakers, and of course, high speed auto racers, make the Bonneville Salt Flats a world famous destination. [xlix] I couldn't get too close because they were setting up for an event and had closed off the road. I also resisted the temptation to drive the Mustang off the road and onto the salt itself. The surface appears hard but in places it can be just a thin crust with sticky mud underneath. Being quite a heavy car, I didn't like the idea of having to explain to the hire company what their Mustang was doing off road stuck up to its axles in mud. The salt flats are an eerie place. Small wonder that they have become so famous and iconic. I spent some time that evening booking up some more nights and ironing out my route through Yellowstone. This allowed me to save some miles and give me more time to explore.

Leaving the salt flats behind, I motored past Salt Lake City and straight through the corner of Idaho without stopping. The scenery I found boring all day until reaching Wyoming. The weather matched the scenery, it was dull and it rained for the first time since I had reached the USA. My motel for the night was in Jackson, where I filled the car with petrol and got some fried chicken to eat. Jackson Hole is encompassed on all sides by mountain barriers. The hole - or valley - is 48 miles long and for the most part, six to eight miles wide, embracing an area of approximately 400 square miles. It lies a few miles west of the Continental Divide and occupies the central portion of the headwaters of the Snake River. Mountain streams converge radically toward it from the surrounding highlands, and the Snake River receives these as it flows through the valley. With so many mountain ranges within a stone's throw, Jackson is a hub of outdoor recreation opportunity. Wildlife watching is easy here; elk, deer, and many other small mammals can be found throughout the valley. A plethora of bird species lives in the valley throughout the year including various ducks, geese and even swans. As it is with mountain ranges, skiing is the major winter pastime and Jackson Hole Mountain Resort, Snow King and Grand Targhee all offer an excellent skiing.[1] It was the best Motel6 so far, featuring such modern luxuries as laminate wood effect floor and flat screen television. I always tried to find Motel6 chain motels wherever I was heading as they were easy to book, have branches nationally and were cheap. This one was just the staging post for my Yellowstone adventure.

With coffee to go I was on the road at 08:30 on a day I was really looking forward to. To get to Yellowstone I needed to drive through the Grand Teton National Park. Not being one of the more famous national parks, and because it looked pretty small on the map I wasn't expecting much and was just taking it in on the way. It is actually one of the most beautiful little mountain ranges you could ever see. I had plenty of stops to photograph the very pretty mountains from the far side of a lake, which lapped at the base on the mountains and seemed to run the length of them. It was hard to capture the width of the scene on camera. The mountains and the clear blue sky above were reflected perfectly in the still waters. I tore myself away and battled through the road works again once into the edge of Yellowstone. This place has it all;

astonishing scenery, geo-thermal activity, waterfalls, elk, bison and deer.

I decided to follow the "Grand Scenic Loop", minus a bit of it that was closed, and timed my visit so that I could see the Old Faithful geyser erupt. There is a wooden grandstand built here to cope with the number of people arriving to take in this natural curiosity. The eruptions are so predictable that there is a time of next eruption displayed to inform visitors how long they will have to wait. Water and steam is fired high into the air, making it suddenly obvious why there is a large no go zone surrounding Old Faithful. Continuing my drive I ended up stopping every five minutes for more photos. The storm clouds were gathering and as I left the park the rain began. The ensuing downpour was torrential and slowed what traffic there was, so that I got to Cody in the dark. I had to ask for directions to the hotel as for some reason I couldn't find my way to it using the GPS navigation. I fell asleep exhausted and knowing I had a day with many miles to cover tomorrow. Rapid City was the destination and it was three hundred and ninety miles away. Having said that, today the emphasis was supposed to be on a "sightseeing day" rather than a "driving to cover the miles day", and yet I still drove over three hundred miles to get through the parks and back out to my accommodation.

Presidents

The potential for boredom on another big driving day was offset by the great road and scenery between Cody and Interstate 90 which would carry me East across the huge expanse of the Great Plains. I cruised down I90 to Sturgis. I wanted to go there on the way as it is famous for the Sturgis bike meeting, where thousands of Harley Davidson riders descend on the town. When they aren't there however, it isn't entirely obvious why they come. There isn't a lot to see in the town itself, but I guess the point is the riding in the hills around the area. It began in 1938 and was originally held for stunts and races, but has evolved into being a meeting for motorcycle enthusiasts from around the world. It brings significant income to the citizens of Sturgis, a town of only 6,627 people. It is one of the largest motorcycle rallies in the world. The first rally was held on August 14, 1938, by the "Jackpine Gypsies" motorcycle club, who still own and operate the tracks, hill climb, and field areas where the rally is centred. The first event was called the "Black Hills Classic" and consisted of a single race with nine participants and a small audience. The founder is generally considered to be Clarence "Pappy" Hoel. He purchased an Indian Motorcycle franchise in Sturgis in 1936 and formed the "Jackpine Gypsies" that same year. The Jackpine Gypsies were inducted to the Motorcycle Hall of Fame in 1997. Hoel was inducted into the AMA Hall of Fame in the following year.

The focus of a motorcycle rally was originally racing and stunts. In 1961, the rally was expanded to include the Hillclimb and Motocross races. This could include half-mile track racing (the first year in Sturgis, there were 19 participants), intentional board wall crashes, ramp jumps and head-on collisions with automobiles.[ii] On the way I saw an interesting sign and took a detour to see the Devil's Tower National Monument. This huge naturally formed rock stands alone in the landscape and seems to shoot out of the ground towards the sky. Native American legend has an explanation. According to the Native American tribes of the Kiowa and Lakota, some girls went out to play and were spotted by several giant bears, which began to chase them. In an effort to escape the bears, the girls climbed on top of a rock, fell to their knees, and prayed to the Great Spirit to save them. On hearing their prayers, the Great Spirit made the rock rise from the ground towards the heavens so that the bears could not reach the girls. The bears, in an effort to climb the rock, left deep claw marks in the sides, which had become too steep to climb. (Those are the marks which appear today on the sides of Devils Tower.) When the girls reached the sky, they were turned into the star constellation the Pleiades.

The next stop for me was Mount Rushmore, where five presidents have their heads immortalised into the rock face. Always a firm choice for me in choosing my itinerary, this icon of America didn't disappoint. Although smaller than you might think from a photograph, it is still pretty impressive. $10 buys you far more access to this site than you could ever want. As a visitor only likely to come here once, buying what is effectively a season ticket seems a bit of a waste! I managed an hour or two's hiking around the huge heads and gawping at them from different angles.

The presidents are: George Washington, (1st president) led the colonists in the American Revolutionary War to win independence from Great

Britain. He was the father of the new country and laid the foundation of American democracy. Because of his importance, Washington is the most prominent figure on the mountain. (1732-1799) Thomas Jefferson, (3rd president) he was the author of the Declaration of Independence, a document which inspires democracies around the world. He also purchased the Louisiana Territory from France in 1803 which doubled the size of the USA, adding all or part of fifteen present-day states. (1743-1826) Theodore Roosevelt, (26th president) provided leadership when America experienced rapid economic growth as it entered the 20th Century. He was instrumental in negotiating the construction of the Panama Canal, linking the east and the west. He was known as the "trust buster" for his work to end large corporate monopolies and ensure the rights of the common working man. (1858-1919) Abraham Lincoln, (16th president) held the nation together during its greatest trial, the Civil War. Lincoln believed his most sacred duty was the preservation of the union. It was his firm conviction that slavery must be abolished. (1809-1865). [liii]

Before long I took off to the hotel which I found without problem. There was a bit of a problem paying though as the bank finally seemed to have stopped my card. Their fraud prevention measures must have eventually been tripped after the card had been used all over the world. I booked more motels and worked out my plans for the rest of the trip. I'd completed over two and a half thousand miles in the USA so far and was still full of enthusiasm for the sights to come.

Interstate 90 was now firmly part of my life. Interstate 90 is the longest Interstate Highway in the United States at 3,101.13 miles. It is partially the northernmost coast-to-coast interstate, and parallels US 20 for the most part. Its western terminus is in Seattle, Washington, at Edgar Martinez Drive S., and its eastern terminus is in Boston, Massachusetts, near Logan International Airport. Interstate 90 crosses the Continental Divide over Homestake Pass just east of Butte, Montana. [liii]

Even just following for this central section, for the second day in a row I spent most of my day travelling along it. Another three hundred and forty miles passed under the wheels. The road is straight across the map all the way to Sioux Falls. Bordering Iowa and Minnesota, Sioux Falls is in the "Heart of America", conveniently located at the junction of Interstates 90 and 29 on the banks of the Big Sioux River. Sioux Falls is named for the Sioux Tribe of American Indians and the waterfalls of the Big Sioux River, located a few blocks from today's downtown district. The falls remain a popular local landmark and tourist attraction. Many of the buildings of Sioux Falls' pioneer past were constructed out of the region's distinctive pink quartzite and serve as testimony to the founder's hard work, vision and commitment to community.

Pioneers first staked claims on the banks of the Big Sioux River prior to the Civil War in 1856. Homesteaders continued to settle in Sioux Falls bringing the population up to 2,100 by 1880, making Sioux Falls the largest city in the Dakota Territory. The village of Sioux Falls was incorporated in 1876 and became a city in March of 1889. By the turn of the century, the prairie settlement had grown into a city of more than 10,000. From there, Sioux Falls' population has grown by an average of 10,000 residents per decade breaking the 150,000 barrier in 2009. [liv]

The car drank plenty of petrol while I seemed to be primarily fuelled by donuts, coffee, crisps, chocolate and beer, not necessarily in that order and with the odd salad thrown in as a gesture to health! I didn't do much, just wanting to get the miles under my belt and get some rest before an even bigger day to come, in excess of five hundred miles. Sometimes the motels were pretty remote from anywhere, and I could easily see why having a car in most of America is so essential.

I felt that I still needed to look at the map more and do more research for wherever I was at the time, as I passed through it. However, there never seemed to be time on top of taking in as much as possible and looking ahead to the next part. While I was certainly appreciating the advantages of going my own way and not having to compromise with a travelling companion, I also started to feel the isolation. In cities full of attractions solo backpackers can stay in hostels which provide a ready-made community of like-minded people. But out in the expanse of the

USA and always moving on at high speed, packing in as much as I could, I wasn't sure when and how I was going to get out and have social contact. The days were great, but at night my lone motel routine was starting to wear thin. I missed being able to discuss the day's events with Helen and having her bouncy enthusiasm along for the ride (which she would have loved, even if she did fall asleep with her feet on the dashboard on every road trip we went on!).

Pilgrimage

Another five hundred miles of Interstate 90 finally took me to Milwaukee, Wisconsin. It was weird to arrive in a big east coast style city. I had a couple of nights booked here. It was around this time when I realised an awful truth. I was addicted to Chips Ahoy white fudge chunky cookies. It was pretty harrowing for my waistline. However, I'm a true believer that the first step to overcoming a problem is admitting you have one.

The whole reason I had come to Milwaukee was to make a pilgrimage to the home of one of the world's great motorcycle manufacturers. Harley Davidson's aren't my cup of tea, but you can't get much more American. Having travelled here you can see why their bikes have developed the way they have. The long straight roads mean comfort is of paramount importance, much more so than handling. So I went to the Harley Davidson museum and paid my sixteen dollars to get in. The museum is a decent size and an interesting collection. In 1901, William Harley drew plans for a small 116 ccl engine designed for use on a regular bicycle frame. Over the next two years, Harley and friend Arthur Davidson laboured on the bike, finishing it with Walter Davidson's help. But the bike was abandoned when it was found that it couldn't conquer Milwaukee's small hills without pedal assistance.

Their second-generation machine was much bigger (405 cc) with an advanced loop frame. Ole Evinrude gave the young men a hand with their bigger engine. The frame was built in a shed in the Davidson's backyard with some of it probably fabricated in West Milwaukee's railshops where William Davidson was a foreman. The prototype was finished in Sept. of 1904 and made its first public appearance when it competed in a motorcycle race at Milwaukee's State Fair Park. In 1905, Carl Lang of Chicago, the first Harley-Davidson dealer, sold three motorcycles out of the dozen or so built in the shed.

In 1906, Harley and the Davidsons built their first factory on Chestnut Street (now Juneau Avenue) and produced about 50 motorcycles. It is still the location of the company's corporate headquarters today. In 1907, Harley finished his degree in mechanical engineering at the University of Wisconsin; the factory expanded, production increased to 150, the company incorporated and their first signature V-Twin engine was built.

Production jumped exponentially to 450 in 1908 and 1,149 in 1909. By 1914, production had ramped up to 16,284 and Harley-Davidson pulled ahead of Indian to dominate motorcycle racing. Motorcycles were used in combat in World War I with Harley-Davidson providing 15,000 to U.S. forces.

By 1920, Harley-Davidson was the largest motorcycle manufacturer in the world. They were one of two major American motorcycle companies to survive the Great Depression despite a drop in sales from 21,000 in 1929 to 3,703 in 1933.

World War II was a boon for Harley-Davidson as they produced 90,000 bikes for the Allies. The company survived a downturn in the 1970s and was back on top of the heavy bike market (750 cc and up) by 1990, when it introduced its Fat Boy.[lv]

Having had a good look around at the Harley museum I decided I could squeeze another visit into the day. I drove across town to the Miller brewery. This place is absolutely huge, like a town in its own right, with roads named after the different beer related things. The tour was good and the scale of the operation really hit home while being shown an enormous warehouse. It was explained that far from being a place to store the product as they manufactured it for weeks or months, in actual fact the entire warehouse would be emptied directly into trucks then re-filled with production over the course of just one day. A blur of cans roars along conveyor belts that wind through wet machinery, packing up to 200,000 cases of beer daily.[lvi] Mind boggling though this was, as usual the best bit was the free samples. There were three to try and the berry flavoured beer was particularly good! The beer garden was sunny and enjoyable though it would have been nice to share with Helen, she loves a fruity beer! It was moments like this that were making me realise more and more that although it was great being able to travel at my own pace (and avoid endless afternoons in shopping malls), travelling isn't the same unless you have someone to share it with, even if it's just 'isn't this cool', or 'look at all the elastic top jeans'!

It was time for a change of direction; literally, I headed south and arrived at Indianapolis by four in the afternoon. The journey took a while due to a few delays not seen in the more sparsely populated parts of the country. There was plenty of traffic getting around the Chicago metropolitan area, some road works and a very recent accident. That evening I checked into my motel as usual and had one pint of beer while I waited for some hunger to build. I was now far too familiar with most of the fast food options the States has to offer, but had spotted a new chain outlet called Long John Silvers. Clearly it was a fish variant which needed to be tried – fish is healthy right?! Even though it was just over the road, as is often the way in the US, I had to drive as there was no safe way to cross. Having picked up my food I was negotiating my way out of the car park, which was shared with other commercial outlets, when I demonstrated another issue with the Mustang. Visibility is poor! With a clang I hit a sign in the car park; ironically it was a stop sign. The sign was on a thin grey pole that had blended into the background. The base was hidden from view by my low seat position and the relatively high 'waist' of the car. The sign itself had been hidden by the Mustang's large 'A' pillar as I turned into it. The sign was movable and had been placed in the middle of the roadway. As I hit it the sign slid away from me on its base, much like the sort of concrete wrapped in plastic base that would hold down a parasol in cafes in Europe. I had dinted the number plate and broken the plastic grille. The incident left paint scrapes in the front bumper. I hoped that it wouldn't be too noticeable and was glad that I had taken out a full damage waiver with the hire company. I mentally retraced my steps to the beer; surely that small amount hadn't made a significant difference to my perception? There was no way I was over the limit. One woman turned to look alerted by the noise, but as the sign looked undamaged I trundled back around to the motel and ate my fish supper uninterrupted.

While in Indianapolis I visited the Motor Speedway Museum, which was good, but having a lap of the track as part of the tour was better. The Indianapolis Motor Speedway, located in Speedway, Indiana (an enclave suburb of Indianapolis) in the United States, is the home of the Indianapolis 500 and the Brickyard 400. It is located on the corner 16th Street and Georgetown Road, approximately six miles west of Downtown Indianapolis.

Constructed in 1909, it is the original Speedway, the first racing facility so named. It has a permanent seating capacity estimated at 257,325, with infield seating raising capacity to an approximate 400,000. It is the highest-capacity sports venue in the world.

Considered relatively flat by American standards, the track is a two-and-a-half-mile, nearly rectangular oval with dimensions that have remained essentially unchanged since its inception: four 1/4-mile turns, two 5/8-mile long straights between the fourth and first turns and the second and third turns, and two 1/8-mile short straights, termed "short chutes", between the first and second, and third and fourth turns.

A modern infield road course was constructed between 1998 and 2000, incorporating the western and southern portions of the oval (including the southwest turn) to create a 2.6 mile track. In 2008, the road course was modified to replace the southwest turn with an additional infield section, for motorcycle use, resulting in a 2.6 mile course. Altogether, the current grounds have expanded from an original 320 acres on which the Speedway was first built to cover an area of over 559 acres. Placed on the National Register of Historic Places in 1975 and designated a National Historic Landmark in 1987, it is the only such landmark to be affiliated with automotive racing history.

In addition to the Indianapolis 500, the speedway also hosts NASCAR's Brickyard 400. From 2000 to 2007 the speedway also hosted the United States Grand Prix for Formula One. The inaugural USGP race drew an estimated 400,000 spectators, setting a Formula One attendance record. In 2008, the Speedway added the Indianapolis motorcycle Grand Prix, a Grand Prix motorcycle racing event.

Since August 19, 1909, hundreds of automobile races have taken place, with hundreds of separate drivers winning. As of 2014, Formula One driver Michael Schumacher and NASCAR driver Jeff Gordon are tied for the record for most victories among the three major events (Indianapolis 500, Brickyard 400 and the F1 USGP), with Schumacher's wins all taking place on the Formula One version of the road course while Gordon holds the record for the traditional oval after winning the 2014 Brickyard 400. A.J. Foyt, Al Unser and Rick Mears each won the Indianapolis 500 four times on the traditional oval, and Jimmie Johnson has also won four times on the oval in the Brickyard 400. No driver to date has won any combination of the three major events, with only two drivers, (Juan Pablo Montoya and Jacques Villeneuve), having competed in all three, with Montoya winning the Indy 500, finishing 4th in the US Grand Prix, and finishing 2nd in the Brickyard 400. Villeneuve also won the Indy 500, had a best finish for 4th in the US Grand Prix, and a 29th place in the Brickyard 400. Johnny Aitken holds the record for total wins at the track, with 15 victories (all on the oval), during the 1909, 1910, and 1916 seasons.

On the grounds of the Speedway is the Indianapolis Motor Speedway Hall of Fame Museum, which opened in 1956. The museum moved into its current building located in the infield near the short chute between turns one and two in 1975; its previous building outside the track at the corner of 16th Street and Georgetown Road was razed for the construction of current office buildings. Also on the grounds is the Brickyard Crossing Golf Resort, which originally opened as the Speedway Golf Course in 1929. The golf course has 14 holes outside of the track, along the backstretch, and four holes in the infield. The

Speedway was also the venue of the opening ceremonies for the 1987 Pan American Games. [lvii]

The drive from Indianapolis to Nashville was one of the more challenging. At some points it rained so hard that the wipers would not clear the screen. I spotted an interesting sign and as a result had an impromptu stop at the national Corvette Museum. There were some lovely Corvettes from all different periods, although the Stingray models were clearly the stars of the show. I didn't think much of this museum again until it made the news in 2014 when the floor collapsed dumping several of the cars into a large sinkhole in the ground. It was around this point in the trip that I reluctantly decided that a trip to the Big Bend National Park near the Mexico border was too far out of the way and instead booked a hotel in Dallas. After that I decided that my priority was going to see Monument Valley and to be able to have a chance to relax and reflect on the whole adventure. I settled on Laughlin, Nevada for that purpose as it is a sort of mini Las Vegas and nicely on the return route. I knew it would allow me a final bit of sun before heading home. In Nashville, I went to the Grand Ole Opry Theatre and Museum. The Grand Ole Opry is a weekly country music stage concert in Nashville, Tennessee that has presented the biggest stars of that genre. Founded on November 28, 1925 by George D. Hay as a one-hour radio "barn dance" on WSM radio, and currently owned and operated by Ryman Hospitality Properties, Inc., it is also among the longest-running radio broadcasts in history. Dedicated to honouring country music and its history, the Opry showcases a mix of legends and contemporary chart-toppers performing country, bluegrass, folk, gospel, and comedic performances and skits. Considered an American icon, it attracts hundreds of thousands of visitors from around the world and millions of radio and Internet listeners.

The Opry's current primary slogan is "The Show that Made Country Music Famous". Other slogans include "Home of American Music" and "Country's Most Famous Stage". In the 1930s, the show began hiring professionals and expanded to four hours; and WSM, broadcasting by then with 50,000 watts, made the program a Saturday night musical tradition in nearly 30 states. In 1939, it debuted nationally on NBC Radio. The Opry moved to a permanent home, the Ryman Auditorium, in 1943. As it developed in importance, so did the city of Nashville, which became America's "country music capital". The Grand Ole Opry holds such significance in Nashville that its name is included on the city/county line signs on all major roadways. The signs read "Music City | Metropolitan Nashville Davidson County | Home of the Grand Ole Opry".

Membership in the Opry remains one of country music's crowning achievements. Such country music legends as Hank Williams, Patsy Cline, Marty Robbins, Roy Acuff, the Carter family, Bill Monroe, Ernest Tubb, Kitty Wells and Minnie Pearl became regulars on the Opry's stage (although Williams was dismissed in 1952 due to frequent drunkenness). In recent decades, the Opry has hosted such contemporary country stars as Dolly Parton, Garth Brooks, Reba McEntire, Josh Turner, Carrie Underwood, Brad Paisley, Rascal Flatts, Dierks Bentley, Blake Shelton and the Dixie Chicks. Since 1974, the show has been broadcast from the Grand Ole Opry House east of downtown Nashville and performances have been sporadically televised in addition to the radio programs. [lviii]

Later on I booked the rest of my hotels for the trip. Real life was starting to push its way back into my existence and I started work on my new CV. The idea of going back to work didn't fill me with any joy, but I'd always known that this experience was finite. Unfortunately it was an unsustainable world of free time and zero income.

I couldn't go through Tennessee without making a detour to the Jack Daniels whiskey distillery. The tour was very interesting and the smell of the whiskey filtering through the charcoal barrels was intoxicating and overwhelming. The only disappointment came when the tour guide delivered the news that in a cruel twist of fate the distillery lies in a "Dry County" which prohibits them from giving away samples. Oddly it was still available for sale, but I didn't buy any as it seemed more expensive here at the source than it was from any normal shop!

Jasper Newton Daniel was born on a Moore County farm in September 1850 to Calaway and Lucinda (Cook) Daniel. He was one of 12 children fathered by Calaway. There were many hardships endured by the family, including the loss of Jasper's mother when he was seven years old. When the young man was around the age of 10, his father decided it was time for his son to learn a trade.

With only a scant, but well-grounded basic education, Jasper was hired out to the local Lutheran Minister, who also ran a dry goods store in Lynchburg, TN. In those days, the local store was more than a market. It provided families with everything they needed to run a farm, a business, or a home.

One of Rev. Call's best known products, however, stemmed from a whiskey still he operated on the Louse River near his store. Like most Tennesseans of his day, he employed the ancient Scots-Irish traditions of whiskey-making, but Call had been developing a system of distillation that was unique to his own brand.

In those days, most whiskey that was made and sold was clear in colour or flavoured with caramel, which gave it the amber look most associated with the drink. It was only aged a few days at most before being sold, which made most whiskeys taste the same.

Reverend Call used the traditional "sour mash" method of leaving a little of the mash from earlier brews in the storage vat to speed up the fermentation of subsequent mixes. In addition, he used a troublesome filtering system called the "Lincoln County process" to age his whiskey. He taught Jasper the system along with his other working theories gained by experimenting and years of experience. Jasper, who was becoming known by his nickname "Jack", soon proved he was an able brewmaster and capable of rivalling his teacher.

When war became imminent in the state in 1861, the Minister and his young associate kept the business going as best they could. Jack's youth kept him out of service, his family was like most Tennesseans of the time and involved in the conflict. One of his relatives served with Confederate General N.B. Forrest and rode with him throughout the war. Jack Daniel and Rev. Call managed to scratch out a living from the store and Jack would often transport whiskey as far south as Huntsville, Al. In 1863 during a "Camp Meeting", a lady evangelist delivered a fiery sermon that inspired Call's wife and congregation to demand the minister make some hard choices. They told him to get rid of his distillery operation or to resign his ministry. Rev. Call decided to sell the business to his young associate.

Jack, who was 13 at the time and mourning the recent death of his father, began to concentrate his time on the business and was a one-man show for a while. He eventually was able to hire a couple of people to help him and, eventually went looking for a better place to locate his business.

Jack Daniel found a tract of land in Lynchburg that included a limestone cave and spring. The pure spring water from the cave became the most important business tool Daniel ever purchased. With the War Between the States over in Tennessee and it starting to come to a close elsewhere, Jack Daniel rightly anticipated the Federal government would levy a tax on distillery operations and, at the age of 16, became the first to register his operation with the United States government. The taxes levied on his company's product were something he always despised, but because of his quick business move and the growing popularity of a unique whiskey that produced much needed revenue for the government, Jack Daniel avoided the Reconstruction politics that claimed many businesses in Tennessee.

He always maintained his home-spun appeal to those who knew him and, as late as 1880, the U.S. Census in Moore County listed his profession as "farmer". Daniel was the first in Tennessee to use hot-air balloons as a promotional tool and often fascinated the locals with his advertising antics. Jack Daniel also started the practice of issuing commemorative bottles to celebrate certain events. He generally stayed with his trademark square bottle, which some say he did as a symbol of his being a "square shooter", which was a popular saying of his day.

During the celebrated "War of the Roses" political campaign between Democrat Robert and Republican Alfred Taylor Jack Daniel gathered some local musicians together to form a band for Alfred Taylor. The band livened up the often boring political rallies and became an integral part of the colourful campaign. In 1892, Jack Daniel decided it was time the City of Lynchburg formed an official town band. Before radio or television, there wasn't much to occupy the townspeople in small cities and the town band often provided the only means of entertainment. In fact, it is estimated that as many as 15,000 small town bands existed in the United States in those days and they were a source of pride for every citizen. With $227 and a Sears & Roebuck catalogue, Jack Daniel purchased a full complement of nickel plated instruments with cases. When they arrived three weeks later, Jack began helping to assemble the band. The Jack Daniel's Original Silver Cornet Band, as they were called, began playing at every possible opportunity and soon became the most famous band in the region.

Like his former mentor Rev. Dan Call, Jack, who never married or had children, brought many of his family members into the company and was teaching his nephew Lem Motlow the Jack Daniel method of making whiskey. Sometime around 1906, Jack Daniel arrived at the office one morning and tried to open the safe in his office. He either couldn't remember the combination or wasn't getting it right on the dial. In a fit of anger, he kicked the safe and broke his toe. Daniel never had it attended to by a doctor and an infection soon set up in the toe. The gangrene eventually spread throughout his system and resulted in Daniel losing his leg to the disease. With the illness starting to wear on him, he began turning more and more of the company's operations over to his nephew Lem and eventually deeded the business over to him.

Jack Daniel survived until Oct. 9, 1911 when he died of complications due to the gangrene infection. The Tennessee legend was laid to rest amid ceremony in the Lynchburg Cemetery. By his grave stone was placed two wrought iron chairs. While he was known to have no great love of his life, the chairs were often reportedly occupied by the ladies he had dated in his life.

Lem Motlow took on a job that he excelled at and, like his uncle, kept the business going through state and federal prohibitions. Following his uncle's death, he issued the first black label whiskey in 1912 to go with the traditional green label Jack Daniel had used. The difference being the black label was aged longer than the green.

Motlow had to shut down during Prohibition, but when it finally ended, he reopened the distillery and went back to making and improving upon the whiskey. In 1944, Lem Motlow finally achieved the recognition sought for many years in Lynchburg. The United States Government issued a report to the company that stated:

"Your charcoal mellowing process produces characteristics unknown to bourbons, ryes, and other whiskeys and thus Jack Daniels is officially designated as a Tennessee Whiskey."

For the promotionally minded Motlow, it was one of the best official documents that had ever graced the Distillery's doors. Motlow remained a vital part of the company until his death on Sept. 1, 1947. Like his uncle before him, he was laid to rest in the Lynchburg Cemetery.

The 1904 World's Fair in St. Louis marked the first time Jack Daniel's Whiskey gained official world recognition. The fair had a lasting impact on America. A brewer named Pabst earned a blue ribbon for his beer, a waffle business that was losing money to the summer heat merged with an ice cream stand that introduced America to the ice cream cone, and Scotland Yard introduced the science of finger printing to American law enforcement in an effort to protect the crown jewels of England, which were on display at the fair.

The success of Jack Daniel's Whiskey continued through the years. In addition to those mentioned in the story, the company went on to receive four more international Gold Medals through the years – the latest being awarded in 1981 in Amsterdam.

During the years prior to Prohibition in St. Louis, Motlow had sold an entire warehouse of whiskey to a businessman. When the buyer arrived, he found the barrels, but no whiskey. It turned out that a group of mobsters under the command of noted gangster Al Capone had drained the barrels from the bottom. Motlow managed to correct the deal, but Tennessee whiskey became one of the most sought after during the Prohibition years. So much so that Capone kept a home in Knoxville where many deals could be made with the numerous bootleggers that pervaded the region.

When World War II began, the Jack Daniel's Distillery went into war-time operations as did most companies in the state. The alcohol produced by the company was used as fuel in torpedoes

In 1956, the Jack Daniel's Distillery was sold to Brown Forman Beverage Worldwide, Inc. The same year the company was purchased, they started a black and white advertising campaign featuring the people and town that have made Jack Daniel's Whiskey a household word. The homespun images of Lynchburg began showing up in some of the nation's classiest publications and was a remarkable success. It literally put the City of Lynchburg on the map of the world and continues today as the longest running advertising campaign in American history.

In addition, the Jack Daniel's Distillery not only reigns in its own industry, but is also one of the most visited places in Tennessee. The Distillery offers tours every fifteen minutes and attracts over 250,000 visitors every year to Lynchburg from all around the world. The company's used barrels have sort of become a cottage industry on their own. They are still popular with plant nurseries and home gardeners as planters. In Europe, however, they are often sought by Scotch Whiskey Distillers, who use them to help age and flavour their own blends. You can get your name on the wall at the distillery if you buy a whole barrel of whiskey. Some names appear multiple times, although usually it is companies like Walmart rather than an individual.

The Distillery location is the only place in Lynchburg where you can purchase Jack Daniel's Whiskey, but only the commemorative bottles the company has issued. After 136 years of being home to the world's most recognized distillery, the City of Lynchburg is still officially "dry". The hardest drink available at the lavish bar at the end of the tour is lemonade. [lix]

Motoring the rest of the way, I had been just intending to stop over somewhere near Birmingham, Alabama, but I'd spotted another opportunity to take in some NASCAR history. I'd been enjoying watching NASCAR on television back as home and not realising how far east of Birmingham it is to Talledega, 40 plus miles, I went to see the speedway. I arrived after the final tour was meant to have taken place. The receptionist called through to the old timer who was conducting the tours and he took me round anyway for a tour of just me. There was no getting on the track like at Indianapolis, but I did get a photo of myself pretending to celebrate on victory lane! During the 1960s Bill France wanted to build a track faster and longer than Daytona International Speedway. He would end up breaking ground on an old airfield on May 23, 1968. The track would be named Alabama International Motor Speedway, but the name would not carry on and was later changed to Talladega Superspeedway. The track opened on September 13, 1969 costing $4 million. The first race at the new track was unlike any other; all the original drivers abandoned the track because of tire problems which caused Bill France to hire substitute drivers. The first finish was amazing with three cars side by side with the winner being Richard Brickhouse. After the first race, Talladega would host two Winston Cup Series races a year, one of which would become part of the 10-race Chase for the Sprint Cup. Since the opening year Talladega has hosted many races and has been repaved four times. Talladega would also have many first time winners such as Larry Schild Senior, Richard Brickhouse, Brian Vickers, and Brad Keselowski.

A 4 mile (6.4 km) infield road course was in operation from the track's founding until 1983. Six IMSA GT Championship races were held in the 1970s, including a six-hour race in 1978. During May 2006 Talladega Superspeedway started to re-surface the track and the apron. Construction started on May 1, 2006 and lasted until September 18, 2006. The first race on the resurfaced race track was the NASCAR Craftsman Truck Series on October 7, 2006. [ix]

Later on in the evening a huge commotion broke out at the motel. Peeking out from the safety of my room I could see lots of black women screaming and hollering at each other while the men stood around watching on. Eventually everything fell quiet and in the morning I was none the wiser as to what it had all been about; it struck me as probably the American equivalent to an Essex girl on a night out screaming 'leave it Tracey, he's not worth it!'.

I set off on the four hundred mile drive to New Orleans and didn't stop for much on the way. The huge bridge across the wetlands led me into the city and I found my hotel. It was a change from the usual motels I had been using because I wanted to be able to sample the delights of Bourbon Street and be able to walk back to the hotel. The place had an air of faded glory about it, fitting in perfectly with the vernacular of the French Quarter. I went out for dinner as I was keen to try some local delicacies such as the Jambalaya I eventually chose. I was also very hungry as I had skipped lunch, driving straight through. After dinner I experienced Bourbon Street, although on this night it wasn't as raucous as its reputation made out. Bourbon Street (French: Rue des Bourbon) is a street in the heart of New Orleans' oldest neighbourhood, the French Quarter. It extends 13 blocks from Canal Street to Esplanade Avenue. While it is now primarily known for its bars and strip clubs, Bourbon Street's history provides a rich insight into New Orleans' past.

The French claimed Louisiana as a colony in the 1690s. Jean Baptiste Le Moyne de Bienville was appointed as Director General in charge of developing a colony in the territory. He founded New Orleans in 1718. In 1721, the royal engineer, Adrien de Pauger designed the city's street layout. He named the streets after French royal houses and Catholic saints. Bourbon Street paid homage to France's ruling family, the House of Bourbon.

New Orleans was given to the Spanish in 1763 following the Seven Years' War. In 1788, a major fire destroyed 80% of the city's buildings. The Spanish rebuilt many of the damaged buildings, which are still standing today. For this reason, Bourbon Street and the French Quarter display more Spanish than French influence. The Americans gained control of the colony following the 1803 Louisiana Purchase. They translated the French street names into English, with Rue Bourbon becoming Bourbon Street.

New Orleans in the nineteenth century was both similar to and different from other Southern cities. It was similar in that like other southern cities, its economy was based on selling cash crops such as sugar and tobacco. By 1840, newcomers whose wealth came from these industries turned New Orleans into the third largest metropolis in the country. The main difference between New Orleans and other southern cities was its unique cultural heritage as a result of having been a former French and Spanish possession. This cultural legacy in the form of its architecture, cuisine and traditions was emphasized by the city seeking to entice tourists by showcasing these more exotic qualities.

The French Quarter was central to this image and became the best-known section of the city by tourists. It quickly became a centre of Creole culture that sought to avoid Americanization. Newcomers criticized the perceived Creole fondness for loose morals. This perception was fought by city officials, but persisted as many tourists came to New Orleans to drink, gamble and have sexual encounters in the city's many brothels, beginning in the 1880s. Despite this, Bourbon Street was a premier residential area prior to 1900. This changed in the late 1800s and early 1900s, when the Storyville Red Light district was constructed on Basin Street adjacent to the French Quarter. The area became known for prostitution, gambling and vaudeville acts. Jazz is said to have gained prominence here, with artists such as King Oliver and Jelly Roll Morton providing music for the brothels. This was also the era when some of New Orleans' most famous restaurants were founded, including Galatoire's, located at 209 Bourbon Street. It was founded by Jean Galatoire in 1905. Known for years by its characteristic line snaking down Bourbon Street, patrons would wait for hours just to get a table —especially on Fridays.

Before World War II, the French Quarter was emerging as a major asset to the city's economy. While there was an interest in historic districts emerging at this time, urban developers felt pressure to modernize the city. Simultaneously, property owners capitalized on the wartime influx of people by opening adult-centred nightclubs that capitalized on the city's risqué image. This led to Bourbon Street becoming the new Storyville in terms of reputation. By the 1940s and 50s, nightclubs lined Bourbon Street. Over 50 different burlesque shows, striptease acts and exotic dancers could be found there.

There was a move in the 1960s under District Attorney Jim Garrison, to clean up Bourbon Street. In August 1962, two months after he was elected district attorney, Garrison began raids on adult establishments on Bourbon Street. His efforts mirrored his predecessors', which had been largely unsuccessful. He was much more successful than those who came before him, however. He forced closure on a dozen nightclubs guilty of prostitution and selling overpriced alcohol. Following his efforts, Bourbon Street was populated by peep shows and sidewalk beer stands. When Mayor Moon Landrieu came into office in 1970, he focused his efforts on stimulating tourism. He did so by creating a pedestrian mall on Bourbon Street that made it more walkable.

The 1980s and 90s were characterized by a Disneyfication of Bourbon Street. Critics of the rapid proliferation of souvenir shops and corporate ventures claim that Bourbon Street has become creole Disneyland. They also argue that Bourbon Street's authenticity has been lost in this process. Given Bourbon Street's high ground location in the French Quarter, it was mostly intact following 2005's Hurricane Katrina. A major tourist attraction, Bourbon Street renovation was given high priority after the storm. Despite these efforts, New Orleans was still experiencing a dearth of visitors. In 2004, a year before Katrina, the city had 10.1 million visitors. A year after the storm, that number was 3.7 million.

Attempts to draw tourists back to the city were undertaken by the New Orleans Tourism Marketing Corporation that featured Louisiana celebrities such as chef Emeril Lagasse and actress Patricia Clarkson with the slogan "Come Fall In Love With Louisiana All Over Again." Attracting tourists was vital, as one third of the city's operating budget, approximately $6 billion, came from the tourism industry. Officials saw tourists as vital for economic recovery in the city. A major impedance for tourists were the mixed messages regarding the city's level of recovery. Advertising campaigns gave the impression that the city was thriving. At the same time, New Orleans was asking for increased federal assistance and National Guardsmen to combat crime waves in the city.

The tourism industry received a boom when the 2006 Mardi Gras went off without a hitch. Popular Bourbon Street restaurants, such as Galatoire's, reopened around this time as well. Reopening and rebuilding of popular tourist attractions led to a surge in post-Katrina tourists. By 2009 when I was there, the city attracted 7.9 million tourists. [lxi]

The hotel location was good and I walked home in the dark and humid night. Next morning I went on a walking tour and soaked up the atmosphere in the French Quarter. When hunger took hold once more I went to a place called "The Gumbo House" for lunch. The chicken and sausage Gumbo was pretty good washed down with a beer and followed up with a brownie for dessert. Having had a few days in New

Orleans I was ready to hit the road again and the five hundred and thirty miles to Dallas were all in a day's work! It was Interstate pretty much all the way to the Dallas metropolitan area which includes an entire additional city, Fort Worth, and is huge. As a result there was quite a bit of traffic for a Saturday. The weather was better here, warm and sunny. I stocked up with food and drinks from a 7Eleven as I was hoping to use Dallas to get some job applications completed, starting with emailing my old boss. That took over my time in Dallas, and I was soon setting off again for Amarillo.

On the way to Amarillo I fell out with TomTom and took my own route which looked more direct on the map. The GPS had indicated that it would take nine hours but my hunch was vindicated when the journey only took six hours including some stops. My intention had been to go and see the second biggest canyon in the US. I have visited the Grand Canyon before, so wasn't planning to make the detour and go back this time. However when I got to the motel I spoke to Helen and she was having a bad day. As she was upset we spoke for a long time and I ended up not having time to go to the canyon today, much like myself, she was missing that support system you have when you live with someone (or travel with someone in my case); the need to have someone at the end of the day to unload on. She had found 3 jobs she thought I would be interested in though, so I spent some time in the evening filling in applications online. This definitely wasn't an exciting part of the trip, but something worth thinking about for anyone planning a big adventure. I hadn't really thought too hard about returning after the trip. I wasn't even sure I would return, or be the same person when I did, so I pushed it to the back of my mind and hoped it would work itself out. In retrospect this 'head in the sand' approach wasn't the best idea. Although some people may be inspired to change their life completely by the 'Big Trip', it didn't happen for me. My advice would be to be to devise a plan you're happy with for life after the trip before you go, as it would make the transition into reality a lot easier!

I had to catch up on seeing the second biggest canyon in the US first thing in the morning on the way to Albuquerque. Palo Duro Canyon is a canyon system of the Caprock Escarpment located in the Texas Panhandle near the city of Amarillo. As the second largest canyon in the United States, it is roughly 60 miles long and has an average width of 6 miles, but reaches a width of 20 miles at places. Its depth is around 820 feet, but in some locations it can increase up to 997 feet. Palo Duro Canyon (from the Spanish meaning "hard wood") has been named "The Grand Canyon of Texas" both for its size and for its dramatic geological features, including the multicoloured layers of rock and steep mesa walls similar to those in the Grand Canyon.

The canyon was formed by the Prairie Dog Town Fork of the Red River, which initially winds along the level surface of the Llano Estacado of West Texas, then suddenly and dramatically runs off the Caprock Escarpment. Water erosion over the millennia has shaped the canyon's geological formations. Notable canyon formations include caves and hoodoos. One of the best known and the major signature feature of the canyon is the Lighthouse Peak. A multiuse, six-mile round trip loop trail is dedicated to the formation.

The painter Georgia O'Keeffe, who lived in nearby Amarillo and Canyon early in the 20th century, wrote of the Palo Duro: "It is a burning, seething cauldron, filled with dramatic light and colour."[lxii] As far as I was concerned it was greener with vegetation and less spectacular than the Grand Canyon. It did have one advantage though, because you can drive down into it. Some of the rocks have really bright red colouring and I tried to get some decent photographs of the black car contrasting with this natural backdrop. The rest of the day was pretty straightforward making progress along Interstate 40. The scenery here, for me is 'proper' America, and I love the west because it is really the closest thing to the USA of my imagination created by various Westerns and other Hollywood offerings over the years. I completed the picture with popcorn chicken and fries while driving for lunch. I was really tired on getting to the motel and fancied relaxing in the motel pool. However all the Motel6 pools were shut for the winter (despite it only being September). I found this ridiculous as particularly in this part of the US it was still red hot.

The next day was another five hundred plus mile day, as I took a two hundred mile detour to see Monument Valley. This great valley boasts sandstone masterpieces that tower at heights of 400 to 1,000 feet, framed by scenic clouds casting shadows that graciously roam the desert floor. The angle of the sun accents these graceful formations, providing scenery that is simply spellbinding.

The landscape overwhelms, not just by its beauty but also by its size. The fragile pinnacles of rock are surrounded by miles of mesas and buttes, shrubs, trees and windblown sand, all comprising the magnificent colours of the valley. All of this harmoniously combines to make Monument Valley a truly wondrous experience. Before human existence, the Park was once a vast lowland basin. For hundreds of millions of years, materials that eroded from the early Rock Mountains deposited layer upon layer of sediments which cemented a slow and gentle uplift generated by ceaseless pressure from below the surface, elevating these horizontal strata quite uniformly one to three miles above sea level. What was once a basin became a plateau.

Natural forces of wind and water that eroded the land spent the last 50 million years cutting in to and peeling away at the surface of the plateau. The simple wearing down of altering layers of soft and hard rock slowly revealed the natural wonders of Monument Valley today. You can also purchase guided tours from Navajo tour operators, who will take you down into the valley in jeeps for a narrated cruise through these mythical formations. Places such as Ear of the Wind and other landmarks can only be accessed via guided tours. [lxiii]

Even without a guided tour, the valley didn't disappoint because it is super scenic and just like in the movies! However, the most spectacular sandstone buttes don't last long when driving through; it would have been good to find a fun way of spending more time in this landscape. Having said that, all of Arizona is full of the big road trip scenery which I love. I'm getting the idea that I should have concentrated my time on the west up to the continental divide. It's now certainly my favourite side of the states and provides an intoxicating mix of deserts, mountains and fine weather.

Exploring the area around my Flagstaff hotel, I took a drive to Sedona. There was yet more spectacular scenery. Sedona is a city that straddles the county line between Coconino and Yavapai counties in the northern Verde Valley region of the State of Arizona. As of the 2010 census, its population was 10,031.

Sedona's main attraction is its array of red sandstone formations. The formations appear to glow in brilliant orange and red when illuminated by the rising or setting sun. The red rocks form a popular backdrop for many activities, ranging from spiritual pursuits to the hundreds of hiking and mountain biking trails.[lxiv] Keen to see more than I could from the car, I went for a little walk in the forest. It was very peaceful and the sunlight streaming through the trees created a gentle dappled light. This certainly contrasted with the bright casino lights of Laughlin. A sliver of the Colorado River Valley where Nevada, California and Arizona meet has been transformed into a fast-growing tourist destination and gambling resort in a few short decades.

Laughlin's current location was established in the 1940's with the South Pointe due to its proximity to Nevada's southern tip. The settlement consisted of a motel and bar that catered for the gold and silver miners who dotted the map, and to the many construction workers who built Davis Dam. Davis Dam was designed to help regulate the mighty Colorado and to provide electricity to the Southwest. Once the dam was completed, construction workers left and the motel fell into disrepair.

In 1964 Don Laughlin, owner of Las Vegas' 101 Club, flew over Laughlin and offered to buy the property. In less than two years the motel and bar, now called the Riverside Resort, was offering all-you-can-eat chicken dinners for 98 cents, play on 12 slot machines and two live gaming tables. Guest accommodations were available in four of the motel's eight motel rooms. The Laughlin family lived in the other four rooms. South Pointe was renamed Laughlin when the U.S. Postal Service inspector insisted Don Laughlin give the town a name-any name-in order to receive mail. Don Laughlin recommended the name of Riverside or Casino, but the postal inspector used Laughlin instead.

In 1972 the Riverside Resort added 48 rooms, followed by several additions and in 1986 built the first 14-floor high-rise. A second casino, the Bobcat Club opened in 1967 where the Golden Nugget Laughlin currently operates. In 1968 a third casino, the Monte Carlo opened its doors. Across the River, Bullhead City flourished in the glow of the casino light. Shuttle boats transported customers from the Arizona side of the river to Laughlin's resorts.

During the 1980s a surge of casino construction exploded in Laughlin. The Colorado Hotel (now the Pioneer), the Regency Sam's Town Gold River (now the River Palms) and the Edgewater opened early in the decade. The activity attracted other investors to begin a second boom resulting in the construction of the Colorado Belle, Harrah's Del Rio,

Ramada Express and finally, in 1990, the Flamingo Hilton. In 1987, Don Laughlin funded and built the Laughlin Bridge at a cost of $3.5 million. He donated the bridge to the states of Nevada and Arizona. The bridge carries 2,000 vehicles daily.

Today there are nine hotel/casinos and one motel in Laughlin providing over 10,000 rooms, 154,000 square feet of meeting space, 60 restaurants, two museums, a 34-lane bowling centre and a variety of boutiques, spas and salons. More than 14,000 casino workers now cross the Colorado by shuttle boat or the Laughlin Bridge each day. The city by the river now attracts nearly 2 million visitors annually who visit Laughlin to gamble, enjoy water sports on the Colorado and attend many high-profile special events hosted by the community. [lxv]

After the drive there I found a microbrewery and stayed for a pizza and to sample the beer. The next few days I indulged myself in the relaxing end to the trip I had promised myself. I explored the cheesy themed casinos along the Laughlin strip, which is built alongside the Colorado River. On the outside my hotel was built to resemble a giant paddle steamer called the Colorado Belle. The rest of the time I did some sunbathing to make the most of the weather, since I had spent so much time inside a car, and knew once I got back to the UK it would be cold and miserable!

My few days in Laughlin ran out all too quickly. It was soon time to set off again towards Los Angeles. I made good time so took a detour along Route 66. I realised that I'd driven some of it already on the way from Vegas to Joshua Tree more than a month earlier. I stopped off in Barstow for food and fuel. The driving got faster and more aggressive the closer I got to LA, but I made it through and found the final Motel6 of the trip. In a bit of a daze about finally going home, I repacked my bags for the return flight. The Motel6 internet was not working in the morning to check the flight times. I had a breakfast of last night's cold pizza, I don't mean for that to sound like hardship, I love cold pizza! Before long I could delay no longer and headed to the airport. I returned the hire car without incident, but on heaving my heavy backpack onto my back I crushed my sunglasses in my shirt pocket. It seemed like a sign that my time in the sun was at an end. A hundred and forty one days after setting off, I arrived back in London and spent some time with my sister and new little niece Darcy. Turned out I'd met more new-born babies on this trip than I probably had done in my whole life! I then travelled back on home to Newcastle. As always the flight was disorienting in a way that travelling through the land never is. I was back to family and friends which was great. The only problem being that inevitably, the end of a trip of a lifetime just leaves you wondering what's next, and if you can still relate to your old life. Whenever I think of all the exciting days and amazing places of this time it reminds me of a lyric in the song 'Sit Down' by James. "If I hadn't seen such riches, I could live with being poor."

Reflections

Take the best bike you can. There's lots of chatter on forums about how it's better to take an older, simpler and more robust bike on a long distance ride into the unknown. It'll be easier to fix they say, you can modify it to suit your needs exactly, and if it's less expensive, less of a disaster if it is stolen or destroyed, and cheaper for a carnet de passage if you need one where you're going. They're all good points, but I think given my experience that I paid too much attention to these arguments. Although the bike choice was somewhat taken out of my hands I certainly would change my priorities were I doing it again. It is said that the interruptions are the journey, but if they come on a daily basis it becomes stressful. In our case it very much contributed to the breakdown in communications between Al and I. For what it's worth, my opinion would be that unless you have significant mechanical skills which point you towards a bike with certain features, for example a single cylinder engine with carburettor, then take something modern and unmodified and rely on the overall reliability of modern bike manufacture. A standard specification fuel injected bike should be very reliable, and standard parts are easier to replace. You don't want to find, as I did, that your replacement non-standard air filters don't fit! Fit dual purpose tyres and work out in advance when and where you will replace them rather than carry spare ones. To me it felt good to be self-sufficient in that respect, but road or full dirt tyres are too extreme for most applications and changing between them is a pain. The additional weight, bulk and faffing about strapping them on and off the bike really outweigh any advantage. Luggage wise, detachable rectangular hard panniers (usually aluminium) are expensive, but probably worth it. You can sit on one while using the other as a table while camping. I would avoid having a top box as well. You have at most two arms, so carrying any more luggage up hotel steps means repeat trips. No fun when the temperature is in the 40+ Celsius range and you've had no sleep and have an upset stomach. If you can't fit everything in your two boxes,

TAKE LESS STUFF!!! For example, don't, as we did take spare brake and clutch levers in case they snap in a fall, despite the fact you have Barkbusters fitted so that they don't. Taking a new bike, or one with all consumables recently changed will often negate the requirement for many parts between places which will have them anyway.

Go by yourself. Clearly this is coloured by experience, and there are definite advantages to travelling with a partner. There is a sense of security, but probably more useful is the ability to discuss the day's events, to relay the exciting moments of riding and the things you've collectively experienced. But it is important to be very careful in choosing a travelling companion and make sure you're going together for the right reasons, not just because of a fear of going it alone. Once travelling alone you can make unilateral decisions which suit your interests, wants and needs at the time. There is also a lot of confidence to be gained by the experience of relying totally on yourself. Perhaps the greatest advantage is that it encourages you to meet and interact with new people, both locals and other travellers. This was one of the best parts of the trip. Al and I didn't speak again for several years, although he eventually made contact to tell me about an article he had written about the trip. He was also kind enough to send me links to be able to download the photographs that I hadn't seen.

Go without a time limit. Some time limits are almost inevitable, such are the complications of getting visas through some parts of the world. However, it is worth trying to build in as much flexibility as possible to both cushion the effect of a problem, such as an illness, or just to allow for a detour to somewhere interesting you see along the way. Visas aside, what limited my time was promises to meet Helen in the USA and to return home at a certain point. While this worked out well for me long term, at the time where I was in Beijing, looking to book a flight to my next destination, I noticed that flying to "nearby" Australia was less expensive than getting to the USA. This is not normally the case when living in the UK, and I wished I could have taken advantage of it. Make your plans as open as possible. Some places it was a crying shame not to spend more time there, while others I could not wait to get away. The more open you are to rolling with these fluctuations, the more enjoyable I think you'll find your trip.

Navigation – getting lost is OK. There are advantages to GPS. It saves space over paper maps, easily gives you your place in the world and provides confidence you aren't going to get lost. However, the systems that are useful worldwide are relatively expensive. As we found out they are a magnet for thieves. Also, the time that GPS is most useful is trying to find a specific address in large cities, whereas this type of mapping is not available for many countries outside of the first world. For example, when following one of the three basic routes across Mongolia you could just as easily find your way with a compass as GPS. In additional point I found was that if you share a GPS it tends to make the person with it mounted to their bike the *de facto* lead bike. This may put undue pressure on them for decisions at each fork in the road and make the follower feel less engaged and master of their own destiny. Getting lost, for me, actually provided some of the most exciting and rewarding riding of the whole experience. I might still decide to take GPS navigation were I planning another journey like this, but I urge you to at least consider the merits of going old school! In addition to GPS navigation, we also had a GPS tracker system called SPOT. This tracks your position and displays it on a website that your friends and family back home can view. It also allows you to send basic OK text messages via commercial satellite and acts as a distress beacon if activated so that, theoretically you can be found anywhere. While I have no reason to doubt that this would be useful in an absolute crisis, I think that even in the most remote places we visited, help would have come much more quickly from people on the ground. The major disadvantage however, is that those taking an interest in following your progress via the website panic if and when the updates stop for some reason. As it is satellite and not mobile phone coverage dependent, people expect it to continue working. However you can still have flat batteries or be stuck in a steel ship for three days as we were! I think it is better for the nerves of loved ones that they take a 'no news is good news' attitude!

(Comment from Dad = it was excellent to be able to plot your progress on a real map with coloured pins to stick in!)

Take a bicycle instead. Motorbikes, in fact any motorized vehicle cause complications at borders. Bicycles have no additional paperwork requirements and can be flown easily between continents. The cycling will keep you fit while you travel and still give you independent motion as well as the option to use other transport. Any other overlanders you see in the wilds will think you are a true adventurer and the pace it enforces will allow you to see much more detail as you pass. Not only that but its eco-friendly! I've no direct experience, but if any or all of these advantages appeal, consider going my bicycle. I know I would.

No matter how stressed and tired you feel, don't snap at your girlfriend down the phone from a million miles away. Trust me, you'll never hear the end of it!

Does it change your life?

Well, yes and no. I remember being rather disappointed at the time I returned home that really I didn't feel much had changed. However, a couple of key things did change. Firstly, I successfully managed to change my career. There are pros and cons to my more recent roles as there was with the pre-trip ones, but in general I think it is more balanced and sustainable. How much this has to do with the work type and environment and how much with my attitude towards work and life in general is hard to say. The trip definitely serves as a punctuation mark in my life. I often think of things when I look back as either pre or post-trip. Ambitions have changed, the urge to go on another trip, utilizing everything I had learned was quite strong at first. Over time this has lessened, and other things have taken over in my mind on a day to day basis, such as ultra-running. I have found that long distance running provides some of the same feeling of epic adventure in the course of a day as you get over the longer period during a bike trip. One thing is easier to quantify. In my case, absence only made the heart grow fonder! Helen's support, both emotionally and practically throughout my trip had been unwavering; nor had I any need to worry that she would get bored at home waiting for me and move on. So a few years after getting back, we finally got married.

[i] http://en.wikipedia.org/wiki/Reims-Gueux#Reims-Gueux_Grand_Prix_Circuit_history accessed 28/5/2014

[ii] http://en.wikipedia.org/wiki/Millau_Viaduct accessed 28/6/2014

[iii] http://en.wikipedia.org/wiki/Col_de_Turini accessed 28/6/2014

[iv] http://en.wikipedia.org/wiki/Dubrovnik accessed 28/6/2014

[v] http://en.wikipedia.org/wiki/Mostar_Bridge accessed 28/6/2014

[vi] http://en.wikipedia.org/wiki/Durmitor_National_Park#National_park accessed 28/6/2014

[vii] http://en.wikipedia.org/wiki/Bay_of_Kotor accessed 28/6/2014

[viii] http://en.wikipedia.org/wiki/Tirana accessed 28/6/2014

References

[ix] http://wikitravel.org/en/Istanbul accessed 28/6/ 2014

[x] http://en.wikipedia.org/wiki/Sultan_Ahmed_Mosque accessed 28/6/2014

[xi] http://en.wikipedia.org/wiki/Erzerum accessed 28/6/2014

[xii] http://en.wikipedia.org/wiki/Tbilisi accessed 1/7/2014

[xiii] http://en.wikipedia.org/wiki/Gence accessed 1/7/2014

[xiv] http://en.wikipedia.org/wiki/Baku accessed 1/7/2014

[xv] http://en.wikipedia.org/wiki/T%C3%BCrkmenba%C5%9Fy,_Turkmenistan accessed 1/7/2014

[xvi] http://en.wikipedia.org/wiki/Ashgabat#Notable_buildings accessed 1/7/2014

[xvii] http://en.wikipedia.org/wiki/Nukus accessed 1/7/2014

[xviii] http://en.wikipedia.org/wiki/Bukhara accessed 1/7/2014

[xix] http://en.wikipedia.org/wiki/Samarkand accessed 1/7/2014

[xx] http://en.wikipedia.org/wiki/Iskanderkul accessed 1/7/2014

[xxi] http://en.wikipedia.org/wiki/Dushanbe accessed 1/7/2014

[xxii] http://en.wikipedia.org/wiki/Kulob accessed 1/7/2014

[xxiii] http://en.wikipedia.org/wiki/Kalaikhumb accessed 1/7/2014

[xxiv] http://en.wikipedia.org/wiki/Osh accessed 1/7/2014

[xxv] http://en.wikipedia.org/wiki/Issyk_Kul_Lake accessed 2/7/2014

[xxvi] http://en.wikipedia.org/wiki/Almaty accessed 2/7/2014

[xxvii] http://en.wikipedia.org/wiki/Semey accessed 2/7/2014

[xxviii] http://en.wikipedia.org/wiki/Semey#History accessed 2/7/2014

[xxix] http://en.wikipedia.org/wiki/Barnaul#History accessed 2/7/2014

[xxx] http://en.wikipedia.org/wiki/Altai_Mountains accessed 2/7/2014

[xxxi] http://en.wikipedia.org/wiki/Mongolia accessed 2/7/2014

[xxxii] http://en.wikipedia.org/wiki/Ulaangom accessed 2/7/2014

[xxxiii] http://en.wikipedia.org/wiki/Ulaanbaatar accessed 2/7/2014

[xxxiv] http://en.wikipedia.org/wiki/Beijing accessed 2/7/2014

[xxxv] http://en.wikipedia.org/wiki/Forbidden_city accessed 2/7/2014

[xxxvi] http://en.wikipedia.org/wiki/Summer_palace accessed 2/7/2014

[xxxvii] http://en.wikipedia.org/wiki/Great_Wall accessed 2/7/2014

[xxxviii] http://en.wikipedia.org/wiki/Tiananmen_Square accessed 2/7/2014

[xxxix] http://en.wikipedia.org/wiki/Gulou_and_Zhonglou_(Beijing) accessed 2/7/2014

[xl] http://www.parks.ca.gov/?page_id=631 Accessed 20/06/2014

[xli] http://www.nps.gov/jotr/planyourvisit/desertpark.htm accessed 3/7/2014

[xlii] http://zoo.sandiegozoo.org/content/about-san-diego-zoo accessed 3/7/2014

[xliii] http://en.wikipedia.org/wiki/Gaslamp_Quarter,_San_Diego accessed 3/7/2014

[xliv] http://localwiki.net/lompoc/ accessed 3/7/2014

[xlv] http://en.wikipedia.org/wiki/Fisherman's_Wharf,_Monterey,_California#Current_use accessed 3/7/2014

[xlvi] http://www.ci.marina.ca.us/index.aspx?NID=381 accessed 3/7/2014

[xlvii] http://www.nps.gov/yose/naturescience/index.htm accessed 3/7/2014

[xlviii] http://en.wikipedia.org/wiki/Sequoiadendron_giganteum#Description accessed 28/08/2014

[xlix] http://www.utah.com/playgrounds/bonneville_salt.htm accessed 28/08/2014

[l] http://www.wyomingtourism.org/travelguide/detail/Jackson/31475 accessed 28/8/2014

[li] http://en.wikipedia.org/wiki/Sturgis_Motorcycle_Rally accessed 28/8/2014

[lii] http://www.nps.gov/moru/historyculture/why-these-four.htm accessed 20/9/2014

[liii] http://en.wikipedia.org/wiki/Interstate_90 accessed 20/9/2014

[liv] http://visitsiouxfalls.com/visitors/about-sioux-falls/ accessed 20/9/2014

[lv] http://www.hometownfocus.us/news/2011-09-16/Features/A_brief_history_of_HarleyDavidson.html accessed 20/9/2014

[lvi] http://www.factorytour.com/tours/miller-brewing.cfm accessed 20/9/2014

[lvii] http://en.wikipedia.org/wiki/Indianapolis_Motor_Speedway accessed 20/9/2014

[lviii] http://en.wikipedia.org/wiki/Grand_Ole_Opry accessed 20/9/2014

[lix] http://www.tennesseehistory.com/class/JD.htm accessed 20/9/2014

[lx] http://en.wikipedia.org/wiki/Talladega_Superspeedway#History accessed 20/9/2014

[lxi] http://en.wikipedia.org/wiki/Bourbon_Street accessed 20/9/2014

[lxii] http://en.wikipedia.org/wiki/Palo_Duro_Canyon accessed 20/9/2014

[lxiii] http://www.navajonationparks.org/htm/monumentvalley.htm accessed 20/9/2014

[lxiv] http://en.wikipedia.org/wiki/Sedona,_Arizona accessed 20/9/2014

[lxv] http://www.visitlaughlin.com/about/history/ accessed 20/9/2014

Printed in Great Britain
by Amazon